T0278351

LIVING
WITH THE
DEAD

LIVING WITH THE DEAD

How We Care for the Deceased

Vibeke Maria Viestad
and Andreas Viestad

Translated by Matt Bagguley

REAKTION BOOKS

Published by
REAKTION BOOKS LTD
Unit 32, Waterside
44–48 Wharf Road
London N1 7UX, UK
www.reaktionbooks.co.uk

First published in English 2023
English-language translation © Reaktion Books 2023

Matt Bagguley asserts his moral right to be identified
as the translator of the work

Copyright © Vibeke Maria Viestad and Andreas Viestad
First published in Norwegian as *Dødeboka* by Spartacus Forlag, 2021
Published in agreement with Oslo Literary Agency

This translation has been published with the financial support of NORLA

NORLA
Norwegian
Literature
Abroad

Printed and bound in Great Britain by TJ Books Ltd, Padstow, Cornwall

A catalogue record for this book is available from the British Library

ISBN 978 1 78914 768 1

CONTENTS

DEATH IS FOR EVERYONE

Whatever gives meaning to life,
also gives meaning to death.
Antoine de Saint-Exupéry, *A Sense of Life* (1965)

There are two types of people: the living and the dead. The dead do not live with us. But we live with them. We dress them up. We burn them. We wash them, put makeup on them and embalm their bodies. Sometimes we cut them up. We throw parties for them. We erect buildings and monuments for them. We plant gardens in their memory. In our towns and cities we dedicate parks and sometimes entire neighborhoods to them.

At times, the scale of our facilitation of the dead is so momentous that their final resting places can look like cities in themselves. We decorate them, bring them sacrifices, sing songs, and light candles. We hide them away in holes in the ground. We avoid them and we display them. We try to make them decompose as quickly as possible, and we develop ways of preserving them.

We worship them, cherish them, and are grateful that they show us what we are: the living. We give and we give without expecting anything in return; without wanting anything in return. We fear the dead, because they remind us that one day we will be like them. Death is the only thing they could give us.

Death comes to everyone. It is the most unquestionable thing there is, the only thing you can really be sure of. Even the elements of life we see as the most constant and universal are not experienced by all living beings. Not all of us experience what Kant described as "the sublime" in nature, its magnificent landscapes or formidable storms. Not all of us feel the connection to something greater: a god, a nation, a belief, or true love. Not all of us get to experience the joy of hearing music, or the terrifying pleasure of an ice-cold bath. Not all of us get married or have children.

Not even the very prerequisite of life is for everyone. Some people will enter the world and then leave it again without eating a single meal or taking a drink; some without even drawing breath for the first time. But we will die. That is a certainty, whether we live until we are a hundred or die when we are born.

TEN YEARS AGO, we moved into a graveyard. When it was established, more than a century earlier, the house we later took up residence in was part of a farm on the outskirts of town, surrounded by pastures and forests. But as the town expanded, it began swallowing up the outlying areas. The farm was purchased by the municipality, which used the northern part of the land to build a hospital and designated most of what remained a cemetery. In those days, the hospital was somewhere you went to die, not to recover, so it was only natural to combine the two.

Maps and drawings from the 1800s show large green meadows, fields, and pastures. Photographs from the early 1900s show the house and the then newly built hospital surrounded by large open spaces with tall grasses and flowers, potato and wheat fields, serious-looking people standing beside horses and hay wagons, and winter landscapes with skiers and people riding sleighs.

The number of graves increased year after year, and today they totally surround the original farmhouse. The old barn was converted into a chapel.

To the west of the house is a cluster of deaconesses' graves surrounded by manicured hedges, and a mound, fairly similar to an ancient burial mound, with low stone arches covered in name plaques. To the north, between our house and the hospital building, there is a large area with row upon row of graves. From the hospital's maternity ward, where parents often spend the first couple of nights after their child is born, you can look straight down onto the gravestones. East of our house the graves are interrupted by a small, beautiful grove of towering larch trees, before they continue in their hundreds and thousands. Immediately south—lying in a gently sloping extension of our garden—is the most beautiful, intimate part of the cemetery, where the graves are not laid out in regimented lines but scattered, as if they arrived there in a more organic, disorganized manner.

NO ONE KNOWS exactly how many dead are buried here, next to Oslo University Hospital. There are roughly 13,000 graves that contain between 120,000 and 180,000 bodies—a number equivalent to the population of a medium-sized city, and greater, in fact, than the number of people living in Oslo when the cemetery was established.

The closest graves are barely a meter from our garden fence. Some of them are not looked after; several of them are covered in moss. Some have plants—mostly ornamental ones—that have grown so big they obscure the grave's inscription. For a small fee, relatives can have the graves maintained by employees at the local cemetery office, who, twice a year, will plant flowers—albeit the same types of flowers, making it obvious who has delegated the job to someone else. Other graves are regularly visited by family members, who plant flowers or decorate them with small mementos or handwritten messages. One grave just across the fence outside our house was visited, almost daily in the summer and several times a week for the rest of the year, by a man who nearly always wore the same red sweater and would stand motionless at the grave with his head bowed. Then one day he was gone. Some time later, there was a patch of freshly laid soil where a new coffin had been buried. On another grave, under the name and an inscription that says "Always in our thoughts. Forever in our hearts," it says "Darn it!"—a final message from someone protesting his fate from beyond the grave.

When we moved into the house, some of our friends wondered if we perhaps felt uneasy about living with graves all around us. Our close proximity to the dead seemed especially troubling for those who were somewhat unsure about their own religious beliefs. The believers, however, and those who did not believe at all, had no expectations of the dead—be it their bodies or their spirits— clambering over the fence to torment us. We firmly rejected the concerns of our more superstitious friends, defiantly insisting that we were lucky to have dead neighbors. Sure, it can get a little dark, and unusually quiet, we said. But to have silence in the middle of a city is primarily a plus. Besides, the silence is noisier than you might think. From early morning until early afternoon, the cemetery staff are busy with their large or small—but nearly always noisy— projects. New graves require excavators, grass has to be mowed, and flowerbeds have to be kept neat and tidy using edge trimmers. During the summer cemetery work begins early, so the machinery is up and running at 7 a.m.

Meanwhile, the dead just lie there.

We rarely see them arrive. The cemetery was full a long time ago, so new graves have to be dug on top of old ones. When a grave *is* allocated, it is usually for someone with an existing family plot, or because an old grave was removed when nobody extended the lease. Sometimes we can hear the bells ringing at the old barn, but there is no way to tell if they are ringing for a funeral or a service for the Old Catholic congregation, a breakaway arch-conservative sect that sometimes uses the chapel. From time to time we might see a hearse cruising slowly along one of the lanes, followed by a small entourage of relatives. Afterwards, the only sign of the event is a wreath and a patch of freshly dug soil. It can be several months before a headstone is erected that states who is buried there.

But every now and then, death is right in front of us. Sometimes we will be playing with the children or having a cheerful conversation with friends before we are suddenly interrupted by a funeral procession, with its dark suits, flowers, and grief, passing near the fence. We look away so as not to stare; someone has lost a mother or father, sister, brother, daughter, spouse, or friend. It is not a normal day for them. We retreat.

When faced with death and funerals, this is what we often do. We look down, away; we withdraw. Apparently, we do it for the sake of the mourners: we do not want to disturb or interfere. But what if we don't look away? What if we allow ourselves to be governed by our curiosity, interest, and empathy instead, to find out what's really happening on the other side of the fence?

ALL HUMAN CULTURES honor their dead in one way or another. It is something that separates us from animals. How to do it is a question that everyone faces sooner or later, but it is one we have found wildly different solutions for, depending on who we are, where we are, and what times we are living in.

Since moving into a house by the cemetery, our relationship with our neighbors, the deceased, has gradually changed. We traveled to Zanzibar a couple of years into our new life to say goodbye to a friend who was dying. We were struck by how differently the people there related to death. The crows in the old Stone Town, our friend told us, had been brought to the island by Zoroastrians, who do not bury their dead, as we are accustomed to, but instead allow them to be eaten by birds of prey. During a visit to our friend's sickbed the coffin maker dropped by, and the two of them negotiated the price as if they were closing a deal on a used car, with amicable bickering and fierce haggling. The graveyard our friend was to be buried in was a wilderness: many of the graves were covered in overgrown bushes and jungle plants, roosters and hens were strutting around, and some of the spaces between the graves were being used to grow chili and ginger.

We returned home with an awareness that in other parts of the world death and burial are often dealt with in strange and, for us, outlandish ways. We also returned with a new perspective on our own cemetery—as a beautiful and lively place, a place that was richer and more interesting for its encapsulated grief, its reflection and birdsong, and the hum of two-stroke engines. But our cemetery still seemed quite boring when compared with the colorful eccentricities of faraway places. After all, we thought, in our modern world, we relate to death and burial with moderation, restraint, and rationality.

But *boring*? It depends on the eye that sees and the ear that hears. Our turning point came in the summer of 2013, when the dead suddenly came a lot closer—eerily so, almost like a horror film. The peacefulness of birdsong and gardening was replaced with an explosion of sounds, and an unusual smell began to reach us when the northwest wind blew. White clouds rose from strange-looking yellow machines. The work being done was a cleanup operation regarding a local burial practice dating back to 1958. For more than two decades, dead bodies were wrapped in plastic—for reasons we will discuss in more detail in Chapter Three—which prevented them from disintegrating. When these graves were excavated, decades after the last funeral had taken place, what surfaced was not finely composted soil containing the odd bone fragment, hairpin, or tooth, as is normal after a prolonged period of interment. Instead, the corpses were found to be almost intact, as much of a health hazard as they were foul-smelling.

The plastic-wrapped bodies served as an epiphany. For the last few years, we have been studying mortuary practices: on the other side of our fence, in other parts of the world, and in the past. In the process we have become acquainted with some of the people working with death and burial; with the funeral directors who manage these long-standing traditions; and with those who are trying to change the traditions and encourage us to consider other ways of facing death. We've become acquainted with the people working at the cemetery, those who deal with the cremation and upkeep, those who meet the mourners, and those who work behind the scenes.

Common to all people, at all times, is that death, and consequently the funeral—whether it is modest or grand, lengthy or brief, involving many or few—is an exceptionally important event. Whether we dress up and celebrate with singing and dancing, whether we wear black and remain silent, whether we burn or bury our dead, it says something about our relationship with death, and about who we are in life. The liturgy and poetry, the sorrow, the joy, the catering, the flowers, and the memorials tell countless stories about human culture, religion, imagination, faith, and superstition. The many ways we handle death and departure are testament to our need for unity and tradition and to our collective powers of creativity.

LIVING WITH THE DEAD is a journey through our immediate neighborhood, the 30 acres of what today is Oslo's North Cemetery. At the face of it, it is a rather uniform place, not particularly old, not very important or spectacular. Yet the more we looked, the more we learned about the diversity it contains: not just different people who are buried but different burial practices. There are long-standing practical issues, such as how the dead should be stored prior to burial, the choice of coffins and urns, how new incinerators compare to old—but there is also much to learn about alternative death practices, such as turning the ashes of a loved one into a diamond.

The book is also about death and burial in totally different places to the one outside our kitchen door. We have studied how the inevitability of death is faced in other parts of the world, and we have been fascinated, often by the similarities but even more often by how wildly different they can be—from the carnivalesque atmosphere in Mexican cemeteries on the Day of the Dead to the fantasy coffins of Ghana—all of which reflect not only strikingly different ways of expressing grief and loss, but the ways that death is used to celebrate a greater sense of community.

We also explore how people faced death in the past. When archaeologists dig through the layers of time, they find the remains of those who lived before us. Old graves and evidence of funerary practices can be especially useful for giving us a glimpse of bygone societies—and can often also tell us about quite specific events in people's lives. Sometimes we can ascertain how they died. If we are lucky, we can form a picture of the life they had, before leaving their loved ones, by examining their bones and grave goods. Occasionally we can also get a sense of what the dead, or those close to them, considered most important in the decisive transition between life and the afterlife.

What funerals tell us is a universal story of how important death is to us, and the importance we place on our final journey. Through working on this book, we have become better acquainted with the world of the dead, and have thus gained insight into a fascinating part of living human culture.

1

IN THE BEGINNING THERE WAS THE FUNERAL

"Can you climb?" The latest addition to our family had started to announce his arrival, and after a few long minutes of walking, Vibeke's contractions had become more and more frequent. We had taken the "shortcut" through the cemetery on our way to the hospital's maternity ward, our closest neighbor, at the cemetery's far northwest edge. As the crow flies, our home at Geitmyra Farm is no farther from the maternity ward than the hospital parking lot, so we had never doubted that it would be better to leave the car at home when the time to give birth approached. The trouble is, a person doesn't walk as the crow flies, and not once during our six months of graveyard dwelling had we ever practiced walking to the hospital to ensure we would find our way there when the moment arrived.

So there we were, at 1.30 a.m., stuck on a fence, because one of the many roads that appeared to lead from the hospital turned out to be blocked by tall wire mesh. Now one of us—the person in labor—was hunched desperately over the ridiculous trolley bag we had packed—while directing a not insignificant amount of rage at the well-meaning and ever solution-oriented other as the strength of the contractions increased. "Climbing" seemed like an even worse option than giving birth in a cemetery.

Luckily a helpful woman with a dog came to the rescue and showed us the way. Shortly after, little Waldo was born in an orderly manner, in a hospital bed among the living rather than outside, in the night, among the dead. We cradled our newborn son while looking down on the cemetery below, and our home within it.

WHEN CHILDREN ARE born, the only thing we can be sure of is that sooner or later they will die—though we would prefer it to be later. Fortunately we don't know exactly when it will be, or how.

We humans are not the only animals to mourn our dead, but we are the only ones that bury them. Most other animals face death's transformation—after a shorter or longer period of what might seem like grief—by leaving the dead where they are. The dead leave them, and they leave the dead. We, on the other hand, place our dead in a new category. No longer among us, but with us in our thoughts, and in need of special care.

It could be that our awareness of our own mortality is precisely what makes it necessary for us to treat our dead like this. We know we are going to die, so we spend time preparing for death, both for the dead and for the bereaved. Our awareness of death, and our need to understand and manage death together with our fellow humans, is one of the things that actually makes us human. It is one way, amidst all of our differences, that we are totally alike: all humans perform some kind of ritual or other when faced with death, although we have developed various approaches to this which are related to cultural and religious affiliation.

Death has always been here. But when did we develop the ability to acknowledge it? When did we first become aware that death was universal? Not just a random catastrophe, but something that affects us all. And when did the need for mortuary practices arise?

One possible answer to this question is that it happened at about the same time that we became ourselves. *Homo sapiens*, our own species, may have been anatomically developed as early as 300,000 years ago. We were probably fully developed cognitively, with all our mental capacities and what is often referred to as "modern behavior," at a later date. When that was exactly, we don't know, but the very earliest formal burials we know of—and which we will soon come back to—have been dated to about 100,000 years ago. We have also found several other early indications of abstract thinking and what archaeologists call "symbolic behavior" that date from about the same time, things that point to an expansion of the mind and to a world of ideas, such as the use of symbols. Imagination, artistic expression, the ability to innovate, and our penchant for religion and abstract thinking are also often associated with the exceptional cognitive capacity of modern humans. To understand that you are going to die is abstract thinking at its most fundamental level: I am, but one day I will cease to be.

This is undoubtedly something that has happened gradually. Deep in the sediments of the past, we can sense that other people related to their mortality as well, long before they became "like us" in the way that we understand ourselves as a species today. Outside of Burgos in northern Spain, some of the very first signs of early humans' conscious way of dealing with death have been found. In the autumn of 2018, we went there to visit what is quite possibly the world's oldest burial ground.

THE SIERRA DE ATAPUERCA are not really mountains, at least not compared to their neighbors to the south and north. They are more like a swelling in the landscape, a 9-square-mile (23 sq. km) ridge between the Iberian mountains in the south and the Cantabrian mountains in the north.

José Miguel Carretero Díaz, a biologist and head of the Laboratory of Human Evolution at the Universidad de Burgos, meets us in the parking lot at the foot of the mountains and takes us up the hillside. The lower parts are covered in gnarled-looking holly oaks, a favorite among the wild boars that live nearby and love acorns. There are boar tracks everywhere, and occasionally you can smell their pungent, musky odor. The valley below is covered by thick November fog, and we can only really see as far as the next cluster of trees.

"Death? You're looking for death? There's plenty of that here," says Professor Díaz.

Díaz has a salt-and-pepper beard, Spanish-style, and he wears a black winter jacket and hiking boots. He has worked in the Sierra de Atapuerca since 1986, and when we met him, on his 57th birthday, he had spent almost two-thirds of his life working there.

The ridge itself consists of porous limestone. Once—5 or 6 million years ago—erosion and powerful streams of water formed complex cave systems within the mountains. About 1.5 million years ago, parts of the mountain collapsed, and the caves opened up to the outside world.

These caves were used as dens by bears and other animals, and after a while by humans too. Large-scale archaeological excavations have uncovered traces of human activity and fossils—from early human species like *Homo antecessor*—that date back more than 1.2 million years. They are the oldest remains of early humans to have been found in Europe. It is also here that some of the most comprehensive finds of other early human species have been made, including more than 80 percent of all the fossil discoveries of *Homo heidelbergensis*. Today, Atapuerca is Spain's largest archaeological excavation site, and fieldwork has been conducted here every summer since 1978. In 2000, the entire area became a UNESCO world heritage site.

"We are currently digging on seven different sites," says Professor Díaz. He thinks he will be retired long before Atapuerca's full potential has been realized.

As the sun rises in the sky, the fog lifts, and we see a majestic view of what for millions of years made this ridge so attractive, first to animals, then to early and modern humans: the valley below, the only route between the Mediterranean and the Atlantic that does not cross high mountains. Humans and animals wanting to cross from one side to the other would naturally pass here. A million years ago, the landscape now covered by swaying wheat fields was a rich and fertile area where humans were far from dominant. There were elephants, rhinos, lynxes, bears, panthers, wild boars, and wild horses, along with numerous smaller mammals.

The professor leads us to a small cleft in the rock, and we climb down the slippery wet limestone to a huge iron gate that covers the entrance to Cueva Mayor (the Main Cave). After unlocking two padlocks, José kicks the gate open. Inside, the cave opens up around us. The annual field season had ended four months earlier, and since then a badger had been living in there and using the entrance as a latrine. "The caves have been used by humans intermittently, but animals have always been here," he explains.

Over the years, this cave system in the Sierra de Atapuerca has had various entrances and openings. But they have all collapsed at different times, making many of the caves inaccessible—sealed for posterity.

We know about prehistory, the time before history and the written word, primarily through death. The remains of those who have lived before us—material culture (all the things they surrounded themselves with), fossils, and bones—give today's archaeologists small pockets of bygone times to dig into, like small peepholes into the past.

When archaeologists excavate, they work systematically, removing the soil from the surface, centimeter by centimeter. Sometimes they will get lucky, and larger fragments of bone or other objects will appear under their trowel. Other times they have to wait until the sifting to be rewarded. Sifting is a practice that involves using a metal screen to separate soil and pebbles from what might turn out to be tiny fragments of bone, tools, pearls, or ceramics. Of course, it is absolutely crucial to continually document in which grid square and stratigraphic layer the findings have been made. Doing so allows an archaeologist to gradually see a pattern in presence and practice, and the changes over time. Slowly but surely, they dig down, and in the wall that is left standing as a reference—the profile wall—it is possible to tell the different layers apart. These layers have been formed in different ways throughout the ages, and it is here that one can see time manifested in physical space. Archaeologists call it stratigraphic layering, and the excavation site's profile wall allows this to be seen. The further down you go, the older the layers become.

People have been living and dying in Atapuerca for a million years, and several of the profile walls are many, many meters tall. In the times that the stratigraphic layers represent, death has been just as varied as life. *Homo antecessor*—often referred to as "the first Europeans" and probably related to the older *Homo erectus* who first migrated from Africa—did not bury their dead. They ate them. Or it could have been someone else's dead that they ate. Cannibalism as a death ritual is not an unknown phenomenon, be it in prehistoric or historical times, but in the case of *Homo antecessor*—that is,

LIVING WITH THE DEAD

around 800,000 years ago—there is reason to believe that cannibalism was mainly about nutrition, and not connected to any respect
for the deceased. "The bones we find look like leftovers from a
slaughter," explains Professor Díaz. "The ages of the deceased are
more or less the same as with other prey. Nearly every individual
eaten was a large child in early adolescence"—an age where a child's
body can provide a good meal, but does not have strong enough
legs to escape an adult hunter. Judging by the cut marks on the
bones, we can see that the meat was cut off and the bone scraped
clean. Some of them have been split lengthwise in order to reach
the nutrient-rich marrow.

While we should assume that those eating the children of their
own species may have worried about being eaten themselves, we
have found no indication in the archaeological material that *Homo
antecessor* had any such reservations or reflections. Human bones,
animal bones, and stone implements have been found scattered
over what was clearly once an area occupied on a daily basis, and
where human bones were treated no differently to other bones.
They were neither collected nor placed out of sight elsewhere in
the cave: what's done is done, and what's eaten is eaten. One day
it is a young antelope for dinner, the next day, the boy next door.
Nothing suggests that *Homo antecessor* had a symbolic or ritualistic
relationship to the dead.

However, if you continue 550 yards (500 m) into Cueva Mayor
from the main entrance, you will find another cave that might be
considered to be the very earliest known example of a conscious
form of mortuary practice.

La Sima de los Huesos—the Pit of Bones—is a difficult place
to reach, and accessing it sometimes involves crawling on all
fours. When archaeologists excavate during field season, intricate

logistical systems comprising electric lights, winches, and ropes have to be installed, first to help them get down, and then to hoist the bones and soil deposits up. The shaft down to the cave itself is 40 feet (13 m) long. There, Díaz and his colleagues have found the remnants of what they believe to be at least 28 individuals.

"So we're not just talking about one or two bones," he explains, "we have found entire skeletons, containing every bone in the human body." This is crucial for how we interpret the material. Finding all these skeletal parts, even the tiniest fragments—whether from a finger, a toe, or an ear—indicates that a body was brought there intact. It is thus less likely that the bones were brought there by predators: they will drag a body part somewhere, to eat it in peace, but rarely move a whole corpse. Small bones would also be the first to be crushed and eaten, and thus disappear.

We do not know the period of time in which the dead were brought to the cave—it could have been one year or 10,000 years. But we do know that they were all from the same biological group, *Homo heidelbergensis*, possibly a common ancestor of the Neanderthals who evolved in Europe, and our own species *Homo sapiens*, which evolved in Africa.

Of course we could ask ourselves: over the years, is it possible that these 28 people just walked into the dark cave and fell down the shaft by accident?

"It's possible," smiles Díaz,

but it would mean that a large number of people, during a fairly concentrated period about 430,000 years ago, were unlucky enough to get lost in the dark and fall in exactly the same place, and that these accidents then stopped. The area just outside the cave seems to have never been inhabited by humans. Nor animals for that matter, we would have found other remains otherwise. We've also considered if these people were being pursued by lions, and fell into the shaft while being chased. But, again, there's something about the numbers that makes this hard to imagine.

Another thing that makes this place special is the lack of tools. If people had come here by accident, wouldn't they have had natural parts of their attire, or everyday implements such as knives and scrapers, with them? Archaeologists had been digging here for twenty years without finding a single tool, until one was found in 2004: a magnificent stone axe.

The axe, which researchers named Excalibur, is made from a highly unusual type of stone for the area. It is mainly a red and yellow color, not the gray-green quartz of the axes found elsewhere in the cave system. "We've found thousands of stone tools from around the same period. But never one like this. It's strange. Hand axes were the finest tools they had at the time, quite different to scrapers or knives. We don't have a good explanation, but consider it likely that it was some kind of sacrificial offering."

This is how experts have ended up concluding that these people were put here deliberately, as corpses, by other people from the same group. It could have been a way to get rid of what would otherwise soon become troublesome carcasses—to remove the dead from the settlement. But the fact that there are so many of them at the same location, placed there within a relatively short period, along with the one beautiful example of a hand axe, indicates a series of deliberate and meaningful actions linked specifically to the treatment of the dead. If these assumptions are correct, it is hugely significant. It means that individuals from an early part of the human family were conscious of their own mortality and acted accordingly: they created a burial ground.

ACTUAL BURIALS, meaning bodies buried in the ground—or "inhumation graves," defined by British archaeologist Paul Pettitt as "the creation of an artificial place for the purposes of containing a corpse"—did not occur until hundreds of thousands of years later. In the caves of Skhul and Qafzeh, in present-day Israel, at least ten people were buried in depressions in the ground, some time between 130,000 and 90,000 years ago. These skeletons, which were found and excavated between the 1920s and 1970s, have been important for our understanding of how *Homo sapiens* moved out of Africa, and for our understanding of humankind's development of symbolic behavior.

One of the graves found in the Qafzeh cave—a clear, rect-angular depression—contained an adult and, at the foot end, a small child that would have been roughly six years old. The child was missing both feet, but the grave seemed to have been undisturbed when the archaeologists found it. Did that mean the child had been buried without feet? If so, why? Was it something that happened to the child and caused its death, or were its feet removed afterwards? Are the skeletons in the grave a mother and child? We have to assume that they died around the same time, and—although it is impossible for us to know why after so many thousands of years—we can empathize with the sentiment that even in death mother and child should be allowed to stay together.

In close proximity to the double grave, the archaeologists also found ocher, a pigment containing iron oxide that binds to clay and forms various shades ranging from yellow to bright red. Ocher is often associated with burials throughout the Stone Age, across large parts of the world. It is commonly thought that color played an important role in the rituals associated with burial. Sometimes whole bodies, or parts of them, are covered by this red color, which in other contexts may have been used as body paint or on clothes and other equipment. In the Qafzeh cave, ocher has also been found on another child's grave, where a young boy aged between twelve and thirteen was placed on his back with a large block of limestone over him. The grave also contained an antler from a fallow deer, which was placed close to his head and hands. His hands were probably placed around the antlers, on the boy's chest, before the grave was sealed and marked by several large stones, lovingly and meaningfully, around its perimeter.

EVEN TODAY, so many years later, we can identify with these people who said farewell to their loved ones more than 100,000 years ago, and chose to do so this way. We can understand their wish to care for their dead, and their need to mark the grave.

The graves also lead to a bigger question: perhaps this is where it all began? Perhaps this is where we became ourselves, as humans?

Burials, in places specifically designated for this purpose with ocher and other grave goods, were admittedly still an exception among the global population at that time. There are a few known examples of inhumation graves in South Africa, Egypt, and Australia during the tens of thousands of years that followed, while the Neanderthals in some parts of Europe and the Middle East also buried their dead between 100,000 and 35,000 years ago. But these are scattered events, and in Europe the earliest known *Homo sapiens* graves are from roughly 70,000 years after the earliest burials in Israel.

For a period, between 30,000 and 20,000 years ago, a new phenomenon was introduced—something Paul Pettitt has referred to as "the ritual burial." We are still not talking about a huge number of burials: there are fifty known cases in total from this period, which lasted about 10,000 years. What's new is that the people buried were given a far more comprehensive selection of grave goods, including unique examples of personal ornamentation. The oldest known graves in Europe that we have a definite date for are 34,000 years old, and located in Sunghir, Russia. They are spectacular.

One of them, a double grave containing two children aged about ten and twelve years, lying not side by side but head to head, is a good example. Analysis of the remains shows that both had suffered periods of severe hunger in their lives and possibly serious illness. The ten-year-old had nevertheless lived an active life, but had short femurs for its age that curved outward, so the child had clearly been bow-legged. The older child had weak tendons, indicating that it was less active and had weaker muscles, and its teeth showed no signs of wear, as one normally finds in young humans from so long ago. The twelve-year-old also had a noticeable overbite, which is considered unusual among the early Stone Age communities that these children belonged to.

We do not know how these children were related in life, but in death they were buried together. We also do not know the direct cause of their deaths, but it could have been related to the physical challenges they had. What we are certain of is that the grave also contained more than 10,000 beads made of mammoths' teeth.

The beads had been sewn onto their leather clothes, which had decayed over time. Since the children belonged to a group of hunter-gatherers, who were constantly on the move and tended to accumulate fewer personal possessions than settled farmers, it is likely that they were buried in the clothes they wore every day. The beadwork must have had an extraordinary visual, and perhaps sonorous, effect. In the grave the bodies, particularly the head and chest areas, had been covered in ocher. Both children were also wearing several ivory bracelets, and the elder of the two wore bands containing almost three hundred foxes' teeth around his head and waist.

All of these elements—the strange physique, personal ornamentation, and ocher—are familiar features of many burials from this period. What is most unusual about the Sunghir graves is the scale: there are *thousands* of mammoths' teeth beads and hundreds of foxes' teeth. However, the two children were also buried with something new, something that has not been found in other ancient graves like these. Beside the skeletons lay sixteen beautiful spears made of tusk. These were useful items, normally used for hunting, yet they had been placed in a grave, and thus taken out of circulation in a society where mammoth hunting was fundamental to existence. The two children would hardly have been active in the hunt; they were not the hunters who had used these weapons. So why was it important for them to take these spears to the grave? Depositing these objects, "giving them away" to the dead, must have been a huge sacrifice for the people still living.

The people buried in Sunghir were probably considered special. In fact, it could be the very reason they were buried—at a time when most people were not. Pettitt thinks that we have reason to believe that many, or even all, of the buried individuals we discover from this time period were somehow considered unusual, and that their burials may have been part of a separation ritual which in itself was something beyond that which was the "normal" practice when death occurred. The deceased may have represented something other than strength, age, and physique, but nonetheless equally important to the hunt—an understanding of the world and the forces within it that we no longer have, but that we can glimpse the blurred contours of by looking down into the grave, and more than 30,000 years back in time.

ONE FINAL THING, before we leave the children in Sunghir: their grave also contained an adult femur. A single bone from a third individual. We are not talking about a bone from a different burial of a whole adult body; the femur seems to have been placed there almost like an object—perhaps like the sixteen spears.

Inhumation graves, regardless of what one chooses to put in them or how they are designed, are perhaps the form of burial that those of us in Europe are most familiar with from ancient times, and from other parts of the world. This could explain why we are so keen to find out who the first people to bury their dead were. But the solitary femur in the children's grave at Sunghir reminds us that entirely different types of burial have been the norm both elsewhere and at other times, often in parallel with, or contrary to, other traditions. What happened to the rest of the person who, in life, owned the leg? The burial of a whole body is just one of an infinite number of possible variations.

2

DEATH AS A PRACTICAL PROBLEM

It is always sad when someone dies. At least, it is *normally* sad when someone dies. But death is always a practical problem. What should be done with the corpse? Whether grandma passes away in her sleep, or dies in an accident, or during a confrontation over the inheritance settlement, we still have a body to get rid of; to act upon before it starts smelling bad, before it starts getting in the way, or starts to pose a hazard to the bereaved. While our emotions can be repressed and our grieving sometimes put on hold, the death itself is a problem that has to be dealt with, and quickly. Doing nothing is not an option.

When we die, everything that once helped us live immediately turns against us. A dead body no longer has a functioning immune system keeping bacteria and other microbes and threats from the outside world at bay. The enzymes and bacteria in the stomach and intestines, which normally help break down food and redistribute nutrients to the rest of the body, run wild, and quickly start eating away at the host itself. Decomposition starts the moment life disappears and all organs fail: the moment the body becomes a corpse. A process described medically in seven stages, from the first stage when the skin turns pale—deathly pale, so to speak, or *palor mortis*, as it is called in Latin—to the last stage where all that remains is bones.

This process can be fast or slow, and it is dependent on a whole range of conditions: temperature, whether the corpse is dressed or not, what *kind* of clothes or other material it might be wrapped in, whether the corpse is above or below ground, whether it is in a dry or humid environment. As we will see several examples of, the various conditions in the soil itself are also key to how fast a corpse decomposes, as is the presence of predators, insects, bacteria, and microbes.

Most people who die in industrialized societies today will be transported relatively quickly to a cold room, where they will await burial. In sterile surroundings, at temperatures just above freezing, the natural decomposing process stops almost completely, and provided the corpse is not moved or exposed to significant fluctuations in temperature, it can stay "fresh" for several weeks. If the body is lying on soil or other organic matter—not too dry, not too wet—and is exposed to plenty of oxygen and fairly warm weather, it can decompose very quickly.

The summer of 2020 will probably not be primarily remembered for the warm temperatures in northern Europe, but at the end of June we were lucky to get an unusually long period of balmy weather and glorious sunshine at our holiday home in southern Norway. One day we strolled up the hill behind the house, along an old cart road that passes through a wilderness of scrub and deciduous forest, to see if the chanterelle had by chance arrived early due to the wet spring and the few warm days we had experienced. Just along the road on the left-hand side, we found, to our horror, a dead moose calf. It was lying among the leaves and twigs on the moist ground, but it was also fully exposed to the hot sun. The calf was the size of a large child, perhaps 66 pounds (30 kg), and must have died in the night, or early that morning. Its coat looked lifeless, as though it had lost its sheen and become flattened to its body, and it stared up at us through a cloudy eye. A solitary fly buzzed around its head and settled on its eyeball.

The first thing to happen when a warm-blooded animal dies is that blood stops circulating. Human skin, for example, will become lifeless and dry. Then the body temperature drops, so that in a few hours it will be roughly the same temperature as its surroundings. After a few hours a stage we know well from popular culture, rigor mortis, occurs. This is a condition where the muscles contract and the joints, tendons, and muscles become stiff and inflexible. As the natural decomposition process continues, rigor mortis subsides, usually after one to three days, depending on the temperature. Sometimes corpses that have been transferred to cold rooms are still stiff and hard to manage when the funeral consultants have to dress them for viewing and burial.

The fourth stage, before active decay takes hold, is called livor mortis, where areas of the skin will change color and form red, purple, or almost blue "death spots": discolored areas where the blood has collected. If the corpse is lying on its back, these stains usually occur on the back and other areas that are in contact with the supporting surface. If the body is in a seated position or hanging from a tree, the blood will collect in the hands and feet. If the corpse is lying face down, the face will quickly turn a bluish-purple color.

None of these first four stages of the body's postmortem were apparent to us as we stood over the moose calf, wondering what had gone wrong so early in its life. There were no visible injuries or wounds, so disease or rejection by its mother were more likely causes of death than predators or an accident. We didn't really want to touch it, so we never found out whether it was cold or stiff. However, we understood that because of where it was lying—near to the road and exposed to the sun—it could quickly become a nuisance for other hikers and a potentially long-term nuisance for us. Since the moose calf was on our property, we told ourselves that we would come back with a shovel and bury it before it started to smell. A summer with a slowly rotting carcass behind the house was not a tempting prospect.

But out of sight is out of mind: we forgot about it, ignored the unpleasant task, and immersed ourselves in other summer activities. Two or three days later we remembered it again, so with a spade and a pickaxe slung over our shoulders, we went up the hill. The smell was nothing like as bad as we had feared, but still, as we approached, it was obvious that we were in the proximity of a dead animal; there was a heavy, pungent stench. Bad, but not overwhelmingly so. What we saw, however, made a much bigger impression. The calf's head had been mutilated by a predator—most likely a badger or fox that had enjoyed a welcome and unexpected feast of nutritious brain matter—and the only things left of the head were part of its skull and lower jaw, which were lying nearby.

The party had then clearly been crashed by significantly smaller animals. In the calf's stomach region there were now thousands of fat white maggots, crawling and wriggling as they searched the rotting carcass for food. The air was filled with the sound of buzzing flies, a steady hum like the whirring of hundreds of tiny fans.

The moose calf was already in the sixth and final phase of decomposition. When blood no longer transports oxygen to the body's cells, the cell walls start breaking down from within through a self-dissolving process called autolysis. After a while the intestinal walls rupture, and the intestinal bacteria spread through the blood vessels to the rest of the body. The waste products from this cell breakdown contribute to the smell, the corpse changing color, and not least chemical reactions such as the formation of gas within the body. The corpse will then swell, and the skin can eventually rupture while fluid seeps from the ruptures and other orifices. The resulting smell is a powerful signal to insects and scavengers. The maggots we could see were blowfly larvae, hatched from eggs that had been laid in the eyes, ears, and mouth, and in any cuts or wounds, shortly after the calf had taken its last breath. The fly we spotted on that first day had no doubt already been at work: flies can smell death long before we notice any sign of decay, as anyone who has tried butchering something or hunting on a warm day knows. Larvae feed on soft tissue and produce new generations of flies, eggs, and larvae at breakneck speed, as long as the conditions are right and there is still food for them. These processes in themselves generate so much heat that the larvae have to spread out across the body (and so eat an increasingly large part of it) in order to constantly establish new colonies in areas where the temperature is lower. If it gets hotter than 50°c, they die. Other insects and beetles will also appear during this phase, while larger animals tend to steer clear of carcasses that are this rotten.

Being self-appointed buriers, neither of us were prepared for the moose calf to be this decomposed already. We had imagined it taking all summer, and possibly the autumn too. But as it was now, we did not quite have the stomach for standing digging a hole and moving what remained of the body into it, and all of the close encounters with creepy crawlies that this process would entail. We walked away instead, leaving unfinished business.

Two days later we returned with a bunch of kids who had heard about the moose calf's fate and wanted to see it. Once again, we were considerably surprised. There was no longer any visible insect life, and the grass and surrounding area gave off only a faint whiff of death and decay. All that remained of the calf were some bones, the odd tuft of fur and four black hooves. The whole process—from death to skeletonization—had taken less than a week, at a furious pace and entirely free of human interference or manipulation.

EVEN AN ADULT HUMAN can be reduced to bones in seven days if all the conditions are right—that is, high levels of insect activity combined with warm and humid weather. But that would depend on the person having died on the same wet part of the forest floor, and not being dressed in anything that might prevent contact between their skin and the immediate surroundings. Had the calf instead been an unfortunate walker wearing hiking boots and an all-weather jacket, who, after getting sudden chest pains, slumped onto a log beside a rockface in a shady and sheltered location, the process would have taken significantly longer. Years perhaps, depending on the wildlife and climate in the area. It can take even longer in a grave, depending on the soil and the depth of the grave. In the calf's case, its remains, thanks to the location and weather, quickly became a kind of natural laboratory. An exciting scientific observation site where anyone who wanted to look and learn could attempt the same challenge archaeologists face when they discover much older remains: identify the animal and determine which parts of the body can be recognized, based on the size and position of the bones.

Toward the end of the summer, it was hard to find the spot where the moose calf had been. The area was overgrown, the smell was gone; whatever was left had been embraced by nature. All you could see, if you looked closely through the grass and leaves, were some scattered bones, partially covered by foliage. And so the dead calf became more a source of joy and wonder than a nuisance. Had we found the hypothetical hiker by the roadside, instead of a wild animal, the situation would have been different. We would not have waited three days before returning with a pick and shovel; we would, of course, have called the police and authorities as fast as possible so that the right departments could perform a dignified investigation and subsequent burial of the deceased.

Regardless of all the other thoughts and feelings that arise around death and the deceased—relief, grief, loss, anger, Schadenfreude—and despite the fact that we connect all of the world's rituals and religious symbolism to the disposal of a dead body, the basic principle in most cultures is that a person who is no longer alive, a corpse, cannot occupy a place among the living. It has to be dealt with. In Western culture, we solved this problem a long time ago by creating cemeteries: clearly defined and demarcated areas for the dead. At Oslo's North Cemetery, there are corpses in all stages of decomposition, and ashes resting in little urns, all buried safely under the ground. Traditionally, we prefer to see the body of our loved ones disappear after the funeral, so that we can relate to the memory of the dead, preferably symbolized by a headstone, without having to deal with the remains for the rest of our lives.

Although the before and after rituals can seem quite similar, modern European and North American mortuary practices revolve around two entirely distinct ways to dispose of the body: burying or burning—rotting or cremation. To soil or to ash. These are the most common options, but they are not the only ones available to us. If we look up and beyond our national borders and time horizons, there are radically different ways of dealing with death. One of them is to preserve. We are all familiar with the Egyptian mummies, and Vladimir Lenin, who lies under a sheet of glass, presented as a modern-day god, in his Moscow mausoleum. In Sulawesi, Indonesia, they have a tradition of mummifying their dead and living with them for several years, before moving them to their final resting place in a mountain cave, where the embalmed corpses keep each other company.

IN SOME OTHER CULTURES, the most respectful way to treat the dead is to distribute parts of the body, as personal mementos, to reaffirm important relationships, or for use in religious ceremonies. To use a bone as a straw, as they do in Bhutan on certain occasions, is entirely alien to Western traditions. But there are several recent examples of corpses being divided up in Europe, too. The explorer David Livingstone is buried both under a tree in Zambia, where his heart lies, and in Westminster Abbey in London, where the rest of his body is buried in the most prominent place in the church.

We can also consume the dead. Cannibalism is today seen as one of the most universal of taboos. But the caves in Atapuerca, along with a series of other archaeological finds, attest to other periods of humankind's existence when cannibalism was not uncommon, both as a means of sustenance and as a cultural and symbolic practice. It is also known to have been practiced in more modern times, in places such as remote parts of Papua New Guinea.

Finally, we can transform the dead. Those who wear parts of their relatives as jewelry can maintain a relationship with the deceased or project a distinct authority. During the last century, the Melanesian Trobrianders made necklaces from which they hung the jawbones of their dead as part of the mourning process. More recently, in Europe and the United States it has become possible to send the deceased's ashes to be processed in a pressure chamber and have them returned to you as diamonds.

Burn, bury, preserve, consume, distribute, and transform: six practical ways of dealing with death. But within each of these are infinite possibilities for variation, some of which we will look at in this book.

WHEN OSLO NORTH CEMETERY was established at the end of the 1800s, it was mainly in response to a practical problem: the capital, Christiania (as it was then called), was growing rapidly. Its population had increased from around 15,000 inhabitants in 1800—if you include the suburbs that later became part of the city—to 30,000 in 1850, and this growth continued at a tremendous rate. By the turn of the century, the figure was more than 250,000. Such an explosion in living residents inevitably led to a corresponding explosion in the number of dead, albeit a few decades later. The population growth led to more overcrowding and a decline in sanitation, which contributed greatly to a number of epidemics in the 1800s. These epidemics in turn led to further waves of deaths. When a cholera epidemic struck in the 1830s, a cemetery was hastily built on the west bank of Oslo's Aker River, at a practical and appropriate distance from the local hospital (which, as mentioned, did not really provide care for the sick but offered them somewhere to die away from the rest of the populace). However, the cemetery's topsoil was inherently waterlogged, so the bodies thrown into the graves did not properly decompose. As the cemetery was right next to the sometimes overflowing river, in the middle of the city's most densely populated area, this was a source of particular concern. Cemeteries, it was agreed, should be located outside the city center, far away from people.

Thus, when Geitmyra Farm went up for sale in 1883, it was bought by the municipality—not because they wanted the actual farm, but because it comprised several hundred acres of land at a reasonable distance from the city. The area was still logistically manageable to reach, but it was far enough away that should the cemetery develop any problems, they would not be a nuisance for the city's inhabitants.

3

PACKED IN PLASTIC

It is natural to think that living in a cemetery is quiet and peaceful. And it can be. During winter when the trees are bare, we can just make out the rush of traffic from the busy ring road a few hundred yards away. The sound of a wailing ambulance siren or a roaring motorbike will sometimes cut through, then disappear. When there is a light northerly breeze, we hear a quiet hum from the ventilation fans on the hospital roof. But we are never burdened by the sounds of living neighbors, like most city dwellers are; we're not disturbed by their bad music taste, or their noisy, never-ending DIY projects. On bright spring days, we can sit out in the garden and marvel at the variety of birdsong as if we were in the countryside. Few places besides tropical rainforests have a greater diversity of bird species than the deciduous forest vegetation found in our neighboring cemetery, and many other cemeteries.

But the silence is regularly interrupted. Now and then the air ambulance, which has a landing pad at the hospital on the other side of the cemetery, will arrive. And it is not entirely true to say that our immediate neighbors in the actual cemetery are quiet. The cemetery is both a resting place and a workplace. During the growing season, rarely a day goes by without the cemetery staff starting a new project that involves a tractor or a lift or a chainsaw or a two-stroke engine.

Nothing, however, compares to the summer of 2013, when the usual sounds of the cemetery were interrupted by an almost constant screeching. Imagine a dentist's drill—a very large and insanely loud dentist's drill—and you'll get the picture.

In the cemetery we could see a piece of equipment made up of a large yellow tripod with a drill attached. The drill was only visible when the equipment was not in use, or when it was being moved between graves. When it arrived at a new grave, it would be covered with a plastic sheet. There would then be a deafening squeal, as if a long-buried evil spirit or vampire was being executed, and for a few seconds a white cloud would surround the equipment. After that, the drill was moved a foot or so to the side and another hole was drilled, then another, then another. Then on to the next grave. And the next. Day after day, week after week, month after month, there was drilling from early in the morning until late in the afternoon. It was a noise that—quite literally—shook you to your bones.

A CEMETERY'S FUNCTION is twofold. First of all, it must look after and care for the deceased. According to ancient Christian tradition, the body will be resurrected on Judgment Day, and it must be intact, undisturbed—like some kind of rose-tinted version of a zombie film. Burial was temporary, but resurrection on Judgment Day was imagined not as a metaphor but as something concrete and physical. Although religious notions of an actual resurrection no longer mean that much for most people, the idea persists that a cemetery is a place where our dead find peace, something we occasionally refer to and think of as "eternal rest."

Second, and at the same time as being perceived as a place of rest and safekeeping, the cemetery is also somewhere bodies are placed in order for them to disappear. The coffin is lowered into the ground, whole, shiny, and beautiful, containing a well-groomed corpse, flowers, and a final farewell: "Ashes to ashes, dust to dust." There, under the soil, the coffin and the corpse will be consumed by the earth, and slowly vanish. The deceased are then gradually forgotten, and if the family stops visiting or paying for the plot, the grave will cease to belong to the corpse; it will return to the community, be designated a new corpse, and a new grave will be dug. This means that the cemetery is also a kind of compost heap.

To ensure successful decomposition, special requirements are placed on the material that a coffin can be made of. Certain ethnic groups and religious communities require metal or cement coffins for their dead, for which special arrangements have to be made, and often result in a grave that can never be reused. Most coffins, however, are made of wood—normally one that is not too hard, to ensure fast decomposition. Both the wood and the lining must consist of materials that will disintegrate during the interment period at the cemetery. In Norway a grave can be opened and reused after twenty years; by then, all that remains should be a few of the larger bones—a femur and some teeth, maybe—which are placed beneath the new coffin when the new grave is dug.

In the graveyard surrounding us, and across the rest of Norway, there are regulations stipulating that the deceased should wear a burial gown made of an easily degradable material such as cotton or linen. In some places churchwardens or other local authorities have banned dressing the dead in their own clothes. Those places that do allow it often require the clothes to be open at the back, to allow decomposition to begin. The deceased will lie in the coffin, dressed in his or her Sunday best, with neatly combed hair, but you will not notice that the suit jacket has been cut open and carefully folded aside to prevent the clothes from hampering the decomposition process.

Cemeteries are not just built in random locations. When new graveyards are to be built or existing ones expanded, geotechnical assessments are now required to assess the soil, determine the groundwater level and runoff, and otherwise determine whether the area is fit for purpose.

Had such requirements been in place when Oslo's North Cemetery was established in 1883, it is doubtful that the land around Geitmyra would have been approved for burials. The area's foremost quality was its location—beyond the city limits and, soon after, its close proximity to the hospital and its constant production of new corpses. In the time before antibiotics and effective vaccines, it was important to always be prepared for epidemics and the subsequent large-scale incursions into the cemetery. They were less interested in the soil quality.

You can hear it in the name, *Geitmyra*—literally translated as "goat mire." A mire or bog is often a pond or stream that has gradually expanded and finally become a large, waterlogged field. It is also an area where the transformation of organic matter is exceptionally slow. In other words, definitely not the kind of environment you would consider putting a cemetery today.

In northern Europe, bogs have been known for their preserving qualities for millennia. Jars and vats of butter, "bog butter," as it has been called, have been found in several places. Most of these finds date to the Early Iron Age—the period between 500 BCE and 500 CE. Quite why butter was ever put there is an ongoing discussion, but the mire's preserving effect and the change in flavor that the acidic and nutrient-poor bog soil produced are among the various possible explanations.

The bog butter that we now find is unsalted, so it would not have kept well for very long in its natural surroundings. However, in an airtight bog with a low pH value, unsalted butter can last sig-nificantly longer—if the bog is cold, at least. Some chefs, inspired by this prehistoric tradition, have experimented with making bog butter for modern gastronomic audiences. The taste is far from what we would today consider "good butter," but we can attest that the new potatoes we were served at the groundbreaking Swedish restaurant Fäviken, before it closed in 2019, offered a strangely delicious taste experience of acidic forest floor and organic tran-quility. They were cooked in the previous year's fallen leaves, with a dollop of bog butter on top.

But bogs have preserved far more things than butter from a bygone past.

Throughout a long prehistory that stretches as far back as the Stone Age and continues up to and including the Middle Ages, people all over the Nordic countries, the British Isles, the Netherlands, and northern Germany buried not just vessels con-taining food in the bog, but weapons and tools, jewelry, clothing, textiles, boats and carts, wild and domesticated animals, and other people. Hundreds of people, perhaps as many as 2,000—especially during the period when much of this butter was buried—were laid to rest in these wetland areas that were neither land nor water, but somewhere in between: the "gateway to another world," as one Danish archaeologist poetically described it. These various depositions—which peat diggers from the early 1800s began finding when they were extracting peat to use as fuel or building material—have led archaeologists to interpret the bog as a ritual landscape for people of the past. All of these depositions (even the butter) could be traces of extensive rituals that took place there—sacrifices to the gods, forces of nature, ancestors, or other mythical beings.

Were people considered to be the ultimate sacrifice, perhaps in times of crisis or on special occasions or other specific circumstances? Was their placement in the bog meant to be seen as a punishment, an alternative form of burial for various "deviants"? Or was the idea of honor and glory the reason for giving someone an eternal burial in a place with especially good conditions for their preservation? The historical source most often referred to, when trying to understand bog bodies, may point in the direction of punishment and sacrifice. In the year 98, the Roman historian Tacitus wrote about the customs and practices of the Germans in the north: "Cowards and poor fighters and sexual perverts are plunged in the mud of marshes with a hurdle on their heads."

Everything that was written as an accurate account almost 2,000 years ago should be taken with a grain of salt, especially examples that were written by Roman historians about so-called barbarian peoples outside the empire. It is an interesting description nevertheless, especially in the details. Several of the found bog bodies have been similarly covered, or weighed down with branches, including one of the relatively few discoveries made not far from our home in eastern Norway.

However, another passage from the same work perhaps suggests other reasons why people were sunk in the bog. Maybe the rituals that took place there—which according to Tacitus were in honor of the goddess Nerthus—were so loaded and sacred that nobody who had been in contact with the goddess's chariot during the purification ritual that followed the parade itself could be allowed to live on:

After that, the chariot, the vestments, and (believe it if you will) the goddess herself, are cleansed in a secluded lake.

This service is performed by slaves who are immediately afterwards drowned in the lake. Thus mystery begets terror and a pious reluctance to ask what that sight can be which is seen only by men doomed to die.

Regardless of whether they were sacrificed slaves or "perverted deviants," some of the bog bodies are in incredibly good condition, many of them with skin, hair, and clothes intact, specifically because of the bog's preserving environment. Some were mistakenly thought to be quite recent murder victims, first assumed to have been buried months, not centuries, ago. Several also had signs of having been subjected to brutal violence prior to being sunk in the marsh. The Tollund Man, who is on display at the Silkeborg Museum in Denmark, still has a leather noose around his neck; the Grauballe Man had his skull crushed and his throat slit from ear to ear; and the Huldremose Woman had her left arm chopped off immediately before she died. Others appear to have had a peaceful run-up to being immersed in their wet grave. Whatever the case, we are clearly talking about a tradition that should perhaps be seen as variations on a theme. A bog burial did not necessarily mean the same thing across the vast area and extent in time where this seems to have been practiced over the centuries.

The bogs in Norway consistently maintain a different pH level than those in the flatter lowlands. This causes soft tissue—muscles, tendons, and fat—to disappear, while the bones are better preserved (the skeletons of Denmark's bog bodies have crumbled, or become soft and rubbery, while the skin, hair, and textiles have been preserved). Recent research may indicate that the human bones found in Norwegian bogs did not always belong to corpses that were put there intact, but were instead deposited as bones, or even as different body parts. Does that mean that an unfortunate owner of these bones was killed and dismembered before ending up in the marsh? Or did someone look after the corpse until all that remained was bones that could be easily picked apart and submerged, some here, some there? Are we still talking about a sacrifice—perhaps multiple sacrifices? Or was this instead the ultimate form of punishment?

Without stretching the parallels too far, it might be interesting to consider these bones in relation to a far more extensive find that was made at Alken Enge in Jutland, Denmark. It was at Alken Enge that a large army—probably comprising 380 (or more) young and adult men, most of them clearly marked by violence and fighting—was apparently slain. It appears that the corpses were left on the battlefield for a period of six to twelve months before the bones were collected and thrown into the river, sometime around the beginning of the Common Era. Grotesque finds, such as four hip bones from four different men threaded onto a pole, have been interpreted as part of an extensive ritual activity, along with the final depositing of the bones in the river. The bones are thought to be the remains of an invading army that was annihilated by what must have been a substantial group of local defenders. Perhaps these are the incompetent warriors Tacitus placed in the same category as cowards and "perverts"? The desire for revenge and punishment may have been the very basis for the ritual activity and, possibly, sacrifices made to the gods.

Much has been learned about Nordic prehistory through these bog discoveries, and yet the marshes still hold more secrets than answers. Geitmyra, like many other bogs, has been drained over the centuries, becoming solid ground in more recent times. Although the cemetery can also be characterized as a transition between worlds, a place between life and death, we are yet to find the remains of any Iron Age sacrifice here. Considering the circumstances, we still have to ask ourselves, should this marsh, this grazing land for goats, perhaps never have been used as a burial ground? In addition to the bog soil, the areas around Geitmyra—particularly the large field on the southeast side of the hospital—contain heavy clay soil. Under a layer of dense, dark bog soil there is an even denser layer of clay, which is dark gray and slimy when dug up, and compact enough to be shaped into a cup or bowl. So compact that when it surrounds a coffin and a corpse, it allows almost no oxygen for natural decomposition to occur.

The cemetery staff have always complained about the topsoil. Quite ordinary coffins, even those that had been buried for more than forty years, twice the minimum twenty-year interment period, would be raised partially intact with corpses not yet fully reduced to bones.

Because of this it became customary to leave the graves longer and establish new plots in areas with better drainage and composting. When graves have been established in recent decades, things have been done differently. Following an interment, the graves are no longer filled with the same soil. The pile of clay soil is taken elsewhere, and the grave is filled with a more porous soil that is better able to breathe.

Christiania's problematic soil conditions were well known long before Oslo North Cemetery was built. Starting in 1833 and for several of the following decades, the city was struck by the cholera epidemics that swept across large parts of the world at that time. The outbreaks in 1833 and 1853 were particularly serious, when eight hundred and 1,400 people died, respectively, and almost a quarter of the population contracted the disease. The city's poor were especially affected, and the high numbers of fatalities led to an urgent demand for new cemeteries. When the first outbreak occurred in 1833, Ankerløkken, a site just opposite the local hospital that had been established for the sick, became an epidemic cemetery.

"Corpses were buried side by side, with their legs pointing north," it says in the Oslo City Archives. After this there seems to have been a constant lack of space in Oslo's cemeteries, and a decision was quickly made to use the area as a regular place for burials. In 1857, to free up more space, they attempted to clean up the section where victims of the 1833 epidemic were buried. But the work had to be stopped immediately. A despairing letter to the churchwarden from a gravedigger named Nilsen describes a terrible situation: "They then broke open one of the coffins, while I was present, and it was full of the most abominable rancid water, and the stench was unbearable." The soil was "toxic" and waterlogged, so normal decomposition had ceased: "The body in the coffin was dressed in its own clothes, which easily fell apart, but the body was intact, which is why we stopped digging. The bodies might perhaps never disintegrate."

Unsanitary overcrowded conditions of inner-city cemeteries was a familiar problem in other cities too. In *Bleak House* Charles Dickens describes a London graveyard "with houses looking on, on every side, save where a reeking little tunnel of a court gives access to the iron gate—with every villainy of life in action close on death, and every poisonous element of death in action close on life." He calls the scene "a shameful testimony to future ages, how civilisation and barbarism walked this boastful island together." The doctor George Alfred Walker—also known as George "Graveyard" Walker—spent much of the 1830s and '40s arguing that London's graveyards should be moved out of town. In his fittingly (if not all that concisely) named book *Gatherings from Graveyards; Particularly Those of London: With a Concise History of the Modes of Interment among Different Nations, From the Earlier Periods, and a Detail of Dangerous and Fatal Results Produced by the Unwise and Revolting Custom of Inhuming the Dead in the Midst of the Living* (1839), Walker describes the "Green Ground" graveyard in central London as "a mass of putrefaction" and goes on to say: "The soil of this ground is saturated, absolutely saturated, with human putrescence . . . The living here breathe on all sides an atmosphere impregnated by the odour of the dead." Walker's work led to the establishment of a parliamentary select committee on intramural burials (that is, those that were located inside of the city walls), and eventually the establishment of graveyards on the outskirts of town.

The most famous example of unfortunate city graveyards is in Paris, the capital referred to by lovers and poets as the "city of lights," but known to gardeners and diggers for its heavy clay soil. It even has its own carrot, the *carotte Marché de Paris*, which due to the dense, hard soil is not the long and pointed carrot we are familiar with, but round and short like a turnip or radish.

From the Middle Ages to the end of the eighteenth century, an estimated 2 million people were buried in huge mass graves at the Cimetière des Saints-Innocents (Holy Innocents' Cemetery), close to the central market halls in the heart of Paris and not far from where the Centre Pompidou stands today. The cemetery was the subject of endless complaints due to the stench of rotting corpses. The deceased, ordinary poor people or a wider section of the population when the waves of plagues made it more difficult to sort through the bodies, were placed in pits that were 60 feet (18 m) deep and could hold up to 1,500 people. Each pit remained open until it was full, at which point it was closed and a new one was dug.

Eventually, there were so many complaints that in 1780 the cemetery was closed by royal decree.

In 1786, they began moving the remains to the Catacombs. What the diggers unearthed was fairly similar to that which was found at the cemetery surrounding our house, as well as that of Ankerløkken. Several of the corpses, including those buried in old graves, had only partially decomposed in the dense clay soil. In many cases the flesh on the corpse had disappeared while the fat remained, hard and seemingly intact.

Antoine-François de Fourcroy, who examined some of the children's corpses that had this fat, eventually understood the link between their partial preservation and the humid, oxygen-poor environment in which they had been buried. This allowed him to identify a process that, under given conditions, turns fat in soft tissue into adipocere, or corpse wax. It was undoubtedly a major breakthrough, not only for science but, it would turn out, for more commercial forces. The fat was collected and then sold to the city's numerous soap-boilers and candlemakers in the years leading up to the French Revolution. It adds an extra dimension to reading the Romantic poets of the era, knowing that the poems were written by the flickering light from ancestors' wax. "The French are a people of fine sentiment, and they certainly carried the quality to a charming point of reflection in receiving light from candles made out of the bodies of their fathers," wrote *Scientific American* in October 1852. "We loathe the cannibal, but civilization has features which, if not rendered familiar, would be as repulsive as the practices of the savage," it continued.

Back in Oslo, sometime around the turn of the last century, a discovery similar to the one encountered by the men of the Enlightenment in Paris was made: the preserved body of a woman, who after her death and burial, most probably during one of the major cholera epidemics, underwent the same chemical process as the one identified by Antoine-François in the mass graves of Paris. The woman, who was named Maren "of the bog," after a popular musical song of the era, is not a bog body in that sense, but instead a kind of mummy that has undergone a natural mummification process.

Much is unclear around the course of events in Maren's postmortem history, but as an interesting "specimen" she eventually ended up as a popular museum exhibit at the Norwegian Museum of Science and Technology. For years prior, she is said to have hung in a cupboard at Oslo University Hospital, perhaps as a teaching aid, or, more likely, as a macabre practical joke to be played on young students. "Could you fetch me something from that cupboard, please?"

One might be of the opinion that a location in a display case at an important knowledge institution is a more dignified place to house a dead body. Especially if the body on display seems detached from us in terms of time and space, like the bog bodies of Denmark, or the Egyptian mummies that are exhibited in museums all over the world. In recent decades, however, more focus has been given to the ethical aspects of exhibiting human remains. Is it either more or less justifiable to exhibit the body of a person with no living relatives or descendants to speak on their behalf? How much consideration should be given to whether the deceased was able to consent to being displayed? When, and in what contexts, does what we still consider to be "a person" become "an object"? Should it ever? These are questions that museum staff increasingly have to be aware of and deal with, in terms of both the visitors and the exhibits. Many museums make efforts to place human remains at a remove from the main thoroughfare of an exhibition, with more somber lighting and notifications about what you are about to see, or might choose not to see. Some museums have removed human remains from their exhibitions all together, while others try to contextualize their exhibits in respectful and inclusive terms.

In this context, Maren is an example of how death and burial are both culturally and historically conditioned, and that such conditions can change within a very short time, or even by chance or a random change of context. Maren lived in Christiania in the mid-1800s. Her lifetime is not some bygone era that we only know from more-or-less random archaeological excavations. On the contrary, we can assume (considering the time and place of her death) that she and her family belonged to a Christian congregation, which means her burial would have been important to them as a religious sacrament. Nevertheless, only a few decades after her death, she was exhumed, and because she had been short-changed by Oslo's problematic soil conditions, she didn't "become soil," as the Christian liturgy had promised. Instead, she became an interesting scientific specimen and was given a new "resting place" in a museum, accessible to thousands of curious eyes every single year. At least she avoided the fate of being turned into a candle, or a bar of soap.

But back to the screeching machines and their white clouds. It is one thing that Oslo North Cemetery does not have the right soil, but there was an even bigger problem, one that was specifically linked to a sudden change in practice. From the late 1980s onwards, excavators at Norwegian cemeteries were being increasingly confronted by unpleasant surprises when preparing the older graves for new bodies. Where they should have found, after years in the soil, only the largest bones, they were instead finding whole corpses swaddled in plastic, neatly wrapped from head to toe and taped shut.

When these plastic-wrapped bodies first started appearing, it was a bit of a mystery. At first it was just one or two. Then more and more appeared. Eventually, whole sections were being found where almost all of the bodies had been wrapped in polythene. A survey showed that tens of thousands of graves from the late 1950s to the early 1980s contained bodies buried in this manner, including nearly all of the graves in the large field between our house and the hospital. Throughout the country, it is estimated that there may be as many as 350,000 such graves.

Who could have come up with such a crazy idea?

What happens when such a method is used is far worse than the preserving effect of clay and marshland: it hampers the normal rotting and decomposition process. There is no gradual desiccation, or natural mummification; instead an extremely slow decay begins to take place, which then stops completely. With no access to oxygen, the decomposition process is so slow that after forty years there is still a corpse lying in the bag, bones intact and flesh in various stages of decomposition. There have been some dreadful examples of this, such as body matter that was reduced to a viscous paste which spilled out when the bag was brought to the surface, leaving a skeleton with patches of hair and fatty tissue still visible.

A report from Oslo's Department for Burials includes a photo of one of these bagged corpses in a grave just beyond our fence at the North Cemetery. The head and torso are still wrapped in plastic, but you can see the contours of the body. Below, two protruding legs, still a ghastly pink color, are visible; the other contents of the bag had spilled out when it was picked up.

"The worst thing was the smell. The smell of corpses is something you have to get used to. When you open a grave, it sometimes feels like a powerful breath is coming from below," says a former cemetery employee, adding: "But this was something else. I've never experienced anything like it. It was unbearable, the kind of thing that clings to you, it feels like it sticks and can't be washed off."

WE OFTEN THINK of modern-day funerals as ordinary, even a bit boring. There is the orderliness of the cemetery; the modern Western funeral ritual's lack of fireworks, music, and professional mourners; the thoroughly regulated rules for ensuring safety and predictability during the funeral's every aspect, which vary slightly from country to country or state to state but all quite similarly point out the many things that are legal and the few things that are illegal. And while we may like to flout some of society's rules, like speed limits, we tend to follow those concerning death and burial with compliant uniformity.

Nevertheless, in this highly regulated and law-abiding nation we had unwittingly developed a funeral custom that ranked among the world's most macabre. Nobody—not even the Torajan people of Sulawesi, who sometimes live with corpses at home for several years before burying them, or the Zoroastrian Parsis who allow their dead to be eaten by vultures—would think of such a thing. What would our ancestors—who chose ship burials, built burial mounds, and laid their dead in marshland—say, if they were to hear about this?

In the end, the yellow machine with its constantly whining drill became international news, and Norway's "Grave Problem" ended up as a story in a number of publications, including the *Wall Street Journal*.

When the first bagged bodies were discovered, no one knew quite what to do. The digging of these graves was immediately stopped, and any plot containing a plastic-wrapped corpse could not be reused until the state of the grave complied with the regulations. *When* that might be, no one could say. Certainly not in the foreseeable future—not in ten years, or even a hundred. Plastic is a material with at least one foot in eternity. Fortunately, everyone assumed, it was a very limited problem. But how had it actually come about in the first place?

Eventually the origin of this macabre burial custom was discovered. On 21 August 1958, a memo was sent from Oslo's churchwarden, Knut Gamnes, to all of the city's funeral homes. It was entitled "Problem Smoke from the Crematorium."

"We often receive complaints from the neighbors about smoke from the crematorium," it said.

It is a difficult situation because there are private buildings nearby. So anything that can be done to reduce the problem of crematoria smoke must be done. We know that the funeral homes often use tar paper in the coffins to ensure that they are airtight. When it burns, this material creates dark smoke which has a very irritating effect on the surroundings, even if it is of very little significance technically.

Before going any further, it is perhaps necessary to explain the use of tar paper: one constant—but rarely talked about—problem is that prior to burial a corpse can "leak" in storage. We are, after all, made up of between 50 and 70 percent water. Without oxygen and circulation, without active muscles and organs, the body's cells and tissues collapse, and the resulting fluid follows the law of gravity. As microbes break down the organs, bile is released that turns the fluid slightly yellow. As a rule, body orifices are plugged to stop this leakage; however, fluid does occasionally seep out, in much the same way as it can accumulate in plastic packs of meat or fish in the supermarket. And it smells. This can be a problem in morgues and hearses. But it is almost catastrophic if it leaks in the church, or while the bereaved are carrying the coffin to the grave. As a precaution, some funeral homes had therefore started lining the bottoms of coffins with tar paper, which was invisible when you looked down into the coffin, since it was covered by sheets and a bed of wadding or straw.

Tar paper had fixed one problem, but it had created another, and it was this that the churchwarden addressed in his letter. He proposed a solution, and in doing so provided the basis for what decades later would become an even bigger problem: "Tests we have carried out show that a thin plastic sheet is just as effective for this purpose." He then, crucially, continued: "It also has the advantage that it can be folded round a corpse and sealed with adhesive tape, thus eradicating any smell the corpse may emit. From now on, we ask undertakers to stop using tar paper or similar materials in coffins, and instead use thin plastic sheets or other smoke-free materials."

This treatment was thus actually a requirement from the authorities, and sure enough, the more you dug into the matter—and the soil in the various graveyards—the clearer it became that this was a problem on a huge scale. The problem with the bagged bodies seemed almost unsolvable. In some places they tried a temporary solution: exhuming the bodies and digging an even deeper grave. By placing the bagged bodies, without the plastic, in this extra-deep grave, space could be made for a new coffin on top. But this meant handling the corpse and its associated matter, and the practice was banned by the government: "Such a practice . . . could expose cemetery staff to unnecessarily heavy burdens. It also violates the provision that nothing but coffin fragments and coarse bones should be present."

A solution was eventually found by former cemetery worker Kjell Larsen Østbye, who, in collaboration with a local waste-management company, developed the basis for the machine that made so much noise at Oslo North Cemetery. This simple idea involved drilling through the soil into the coffin, then filling the coffin with a mixture of water, air, and quicklime. Thus, the coffin and everything in it would, finally, decompose. After two years, the grave is ready to be used again. In a 2013 interview, the company's manager, Runar Frømyhr, estimated that—in addition to the graves containing polythene—there were close to a million graves where the clay content was so high that it did not meet the requirements necessary for successful decomposition. "The poor soil is not just a health hazard for those who work on the graveyard," said Frømyhr. "It is also unethical. The church promises that 'from earth you came, and to earth you shall return.'"

There are now plans to export this technology to other countries, and not just for use in cases of plastic-wrapped corpses, which are probably rare outside Norway. In Greece, urban crowding has put such enormous pressure on city graveyards that there are reports of bodies having to be exhumed after as little as three years, at which point they are often only partially decomposed. Greece is also by no means the only country where graveyards have been filled beyond their capacity; the same applies for most urban settlements in cultures that practice burial. But if the "decomposition machine" was used, it would enable these corpses to go through this "earth-to-earth" process in a far shorter time.

4

THE BUSINESS OF DEATH

One wet autumn day a few years ago, we noticed a small car stop on the street that passes through the cemetery, just outside the driveway to our house. What made the sight remarkable wasn't that the car had stopped in the middle of a no-parking zone, which happens all the time, or that the driver was quite formally dressed for a Monday, which is a little more unusual; it was the coffin attached to the car's roof. The car's driver climbed out and thoroughly checked all the straps, then tightened some of them before climbing back into the car and driving on.

Whether there was a body in the coffin we don't know, but it was such a puzzling sight that people stopped what they were doing to stare. Some were curious, others shook their heads. One pedestrian turned round and walked along a different route, the winding path through the graveyard on the other side of our house.

DEATH IS A distant thing for most, even for those who pass through the cemetery on their way to or from work every day. We only die once, after all. And death only affects most of us a few times during our lives, when those closest to us die. It is irrevocable— and exceptional. If nature runs its course, without accidents or untimely illnesses affecting a family, a generation can pass between grandparents dying and the demise of the parents.

LIVING WITH THE DEAD

But if we look around, death is always present. Around 60 million people die every year, worldwide. And when a person dies, someone else has to deal with it. The body must be cared for, transported, and placed in a coffin or wrapped in a shroud, which involves a number of small and large tasks. The clothes the deceased wore in the nursing home, or during the road accident that cost them their life, normally do not go with them. Rites of passage must be carried out; memorials have to be held. The body is dressed and made up, buried, or burned—or sent on its way according to other cultural or religious regulations. All this must happen in a way that maintains both the dignity of the dead and the health and safety of the bereaved.

In traditional societies, these tasks are often handled collectively. Some are reserved for the family, while others are carried out by the rest of the village. But even in self-sufficient communities, the tasks around death often became specialized without necessarily becoming outright professions. Among several African tribes, including the Dowayo people of Cameroon and the Nyakusa people of Tanzania, some of the deceased's friends and semi-distant relatives act as "joking partners" during the funeral ceremonies. Their role is to stir things up and offer insults to the deceased, as a way of maintaining the social ties, even in death—rather like a mischievous best-man's speech at a wedding. Some of the tasks around death are considered such a great honor, while other tasks might be considered so impure that only specially chosen members of the community can perform them.

On the islands of Mauritius in the Indian Ocean, the state broadcaster has its own TV channel of religious and cultural programs devoted to the island's many linguistic, ethnic, and religious groups. Flick through the channels and you might come across a pleasant Hindu woman telling you how to cook for the upcoming holiday, while next it could be a visit to a Tamil festival, a procession of Chinese dragons marking the New Year, or the memorial of Father Laval, the island's very own saint, famous and revered but not quite beatified by the church in Rome. Far more surprising was the time we came across the slow, almost meditative coverage of a number of serious-looking, white-clad men performing a ritual we didn't initially understand, involving a sponge and a table covered with a white sheet. We watched this weird spectacle for a few minutes before it dawned on us that there was a body under the white sheet—a corpse that had been carefully washed using the sponge. The program was part of the religious information for the islands' Muslims, where the task of looking after the dead is still to a large extent carried out by immediate family. In this sense, the program—with its instructions about not cutting hair or nails and how to divide and tie the shroud, and its checklists of shampoo, nail polish remover (if necessary), two large towels (preferably not new, since used towels are more absorbent), cotton swabs, and waste bags—was just as natural and useful as the Hindu cooking show with its recipes and shopping lists.

In contemporary Western society, however, death is almost entirely professionalized—among the majority Christian or secular population, that is. When our loved ones die, it is no longer common to wash and care for the dead ourselves. The deceased are no longer carried on the shoulders of their grieving—or relieved—sons or driven by horse and cart from home to the burial grounds. Dealing with death has become a profession, an industry, a service we buy. And although there is no law against doing most of these things yourself, we still stop—or turn around—when someone chooses to break from modern customs and transport the coffin on the roof of their own car.

The establishment of modern funeral services coincided with the industrialization and urbanization of the nineteenth century. By the start of the 1900s they had become providers of a full service that could handle all of the required practical duties, from the time of death until the end of the ceremony. This professionalization means that many people growing up in Europe or the United States have never experienced death at close hand.

"We're expecting things to quieten down soon," says Freddy Hultgren when we meet him in the office of Aker Funeral Directors, one of our closest neighbors, on the east side of the cemetery.

"That's how the business is now. Fewer people die in the summer, so there's less for us to do."

It is late May, and as we walk to our meeting the cemetery is full of flowers, birdsong, and human life. Hultgren's office, however, is quiet, and neither bright nor dark. The room is furnished so discreetly it's barely noticeable. Since moving into the cemetery, we have passed the building, with its stylized logo and distinguished name, hundreds, if not thousands, of times. We have walked by on our way to the bus, the post office, the pharmacy, and the shop. But it's the first time we have ever been inside. A funeral home isn't really somewhere you just drop by.

Hultgren has run the place since 1993, which makes him a relative newcomer to the business. Funeral homes have traditionally been family businesses dating back generations. The last couple of decades have seen a major consolidation of businesses, most noticeably in the United States and the United Kingdom, and those who remain independent tend to belong to networks that ensure them shared accounting systems and purchasing agreements, while otherwise giving them a large degree of autonomy. Nevertheless, a great many of those working in the industry married or were born into it. Many of the funeral consultants we spoke to emphasized how they also feel like part of a family in terms of their profession. It offers them a distinct sense of unity, and a specific jargon, within a community based on shared experiences that the rest of society knows little to nothing about.

This community can also make it difficult to establish yourself in the industry as an outsider—something Hultgren experienced when he started out in the 1990s. Originally a mechanic, Hultgren had a number of different jobs in the car industry before eventually ending up working with imports and marketing. But his dream was to work as a funeral director and run his own funeral home. This rather unusual dream had been with him since the death of his father a few years earlier: "We got help from a funeral director, but the experience felt quite impersonal. I got the impression that many of the funeral homes had become so big that they couldn't follow a family through the entire process."

In Hultgren's opinion, the professionalization of the industry had come at the expense of personal service. Workers in the funeral services had started calling themselves "funeral consultants" to avoid the slightly unfortunate connotations associated with the popularly used term "undertaker," and Hultgren felt that they had become a bit too slick and similar to other consultants.

Gaining the experience necessary to establish himself would prove to be difficult. It is a closed industry, with very few places willing to offer work—not even low-paying or unpaid internships—to someone openly looking to become a competitor. For Hultgren, the breakthrough came when he met a former colleague from the car industry who now worked in the funeral business. They decided to join forces and open their own agency. Hultgren would contribute with his vision and his knowledge of admin and marketing, and the partner with his practical knowledge of the day-to-day running of a funeral home.

The funeral industry is conservative—and that applies not just to the employees but to a large extent the customers as well. It is quite different to other industries, which might reward you for being new, exciting, and different. Furthermore, new and interesting was not what Hultgren wanted to be. He wanted to run an old-fashioned funeral home, where you get personal service from start to finish, offering a tailor-made experience rather than one off the shelf.

How do you run a new establishment in an industry that is unfamiliar with people selling themselves, and where trust and experience are crucial? How do you get your first customers?

The decisions Hultgren made are illustrative. Rather than portraying itself as a newly started challenger, every decision the agency made—from design profile to the discreet marketing he conducted—was aimed at presenting this new funeral home as well established and safe. Even the name itself, "Aker," refers to the old name of the rural pastureland that at one time surrounded, and is now a part of, the capital. It gives the impression of a respected company with deep roots in the local community, but, as Hultgren goes on to say:

It also helped that the name began with the letter A. When we opened, funeral homes had recently been forbidden from leaving their brochures in local hospitals and nursing homes. After some unfortunate situations, where some felt that some funeral homes were marketing themselves a bit

too aggressively, a shared and neutral list, which included
the names of all the funeral homes, was prepared instead.
That's where the A came in. To be first on that list was clearly
an advantage. We had also opened in time to get on the first
list. The same went for the telephone directory, which at
the time was a very important part of business marketing.

Nevertheless, the initial period was demanding for the new
funeral home. During their first months of business, they had
no customers. Not one. With few opportunities to advertise or
make himself known, Freddy Hultgren took to driving his newly
purchased hearse around during rush hour:

> I made a special point of crossing the busy junction at Carl
> Berners Plass, where the traffic was jammed solid every day
> at the same time. I figured that if I made my way across the
> junction, then drove back, and then back again, hundreds of
> people would see the car and the logo every day. Perhaps that
> would grab someone's attention, I thought. And it couldn't
> do any harm. It was better than sitting and waiting beside a
> phone that never rang.

We had always thought that the location of their office had
been chosen because of its close proximity to the cemetery—that it
was strategic. Hultgren explains, however, that for him the decisive
factor was not the cemetery but the location next to a busy round-
about. Every day, thousands of cars, buses, and bicycles pass by,
and like the trips he made over the Carl Berner junction, the idea is
that these passers-by will remember the name, make a subconscious
note of it, and when the time comes for any of their loved ones in

the months, years, or decades ahead, there is a chance that they will think of Aker Funeral Directors.

The company had its first customer about six months after they opened. Almost eight years after deciding to become a funeral director, Hultgren could finally say that he was one. "It's never monotonous work," he notes.

From the outside, wearing a dark suit every day, always being in the background, always maneuvering quietly between people in mourning, might seem boring and routine:

> There are constantly new challenges concerning the bereaved, or practical things, such as having to repatriate a body, or dealing with people with other cultural backgrounds who want totally different things from a funeral than we are used to. Even "ordinary" funerals vary, simply because people are different and you get close to them.

Today, Hultgren is an institution within the business, known among his peers as a custodian of the gold standard for traditional funerals. The hearse is always washed between funerals. Candlesticks must be free of grease stains or drops of candle wax. And, not least, Hultgren insists on the principle that the bereaved must always have the same point of contact at the funeral home, from the first meeting until the final invoice.

That funerals are a commercial service is an obvious truth that is often somewhat hard to deal with. In Norway, many funeral-related services are directly or indirectly subsidized by the authorities, who—for social or cultural reasons, or in the interests of health and hygiene—work to ensure that a dignified burial is possible for everyone, regardless of their economic and social circumstances. Graves, for example, are provided free of charge for the first twenty years. In Oslo and several other municipalities, the cremation fee has been dropped for local residents in order to encourage this space-saving practice, and if the deceased has to be transported more than 12 miles (20 km) there are separate government support schemes that will assist. Beyond that, funeral homes are commercial entities operating in a market. They are, in many respects, not so different from used-car dealers or bakeries, apart from the important fact that they deal with funerals, not the sale of vehicles or cupcakes. But all the overheads have to be covered, and every working hour paid for, along with rental expenses, municipal taxes, equipment costs, parking charges, maintenance, and trade-organization membership fees. So the way to solve this is to charge for your services and resell goods at a higher price than you bought them for.

"The invoices are especially important," explains Hultgren:

Funerals are a service that we sell, and we need to get paid. But it's also a question of trust. In all business, and particularly ours, it's extremely important to avoid misunderstandings. When we arrange a funeral there are often several rounds during which the bereaved will make up their minds, then change their minds, and then change their minds again. And if several people all need to have an overview, this will inevitably cause confusion—small or large misunderstandings, an extra item on the invoice that was supposed to have been removed, or an item billed twice that can lead to additional problems, lack of trust, and even bitterness later on.

In some countries, the government support for funerals is minimal. It is a choice between a publicly funded place in an unmarked pauper's grave, with all the associated shame and social stigma, and a funeral where all, or nearly all, of the expenses have to be covered by the deceased's family. That can quickly become expensive—especially when someone wants to make a profit on all the small and large items on the bill. The cartoon version of a funeral consultant is a hollow-cheeked man dressed in black, with a uniquely foreboding presence. He will often have a vulture perched on the shoulder, as if to symbolize that the two are one and the same.

This caricature is not so far removed from the image that we encounter in Jessica Mitford's 1963 book *The American Way of Death* (revised and updated before the author's own death in 1996). Mitford was an upper-class English woman, one of the "Mitford sisters." While one sister, Nancy, moved to Versailles, France, where she wrote novels and conducted a long-standing affair with a prominent Gaullist politician, and her other sisters, Diana and Unity, dedicated themselves to Hitler and the creation of a fascist state in Britain, Jessica left her privileged background for a life as an activist in the United States. Her second husband was the civil rights lawyer Robert Treuhaft, who represented a number of low-income clients. What many of these clients had in common was that a death in the family—often that of the breadwinner—had brought not only grief and loss of future income, but a third catastrophe: the expense of a funeral. This became the starting point for Mitford's examination of the industry. She wanted to find out what was going on behind the scenes.

Reading Mitford's prose today is still a pleasure, despite the incredible number of details, particularly regarding costs. The book relays how the funeral industry—perhaps especially in the United

States—was at the time excessively secretive, an industry that pretended it was not profit-driven yet was, to a large extent, founded on deceiving its customers. The book landed on the American public like a bomb and has had consequences far beyond the country's borders.

Large parts of *The American Way of Death* are concerned with how various commercial operators in America's funeral industry force or trick ordinary people into spending far more money on funerals than should be necessary, using devious sales techniques that are totally invisible to their clients. This largely concerns the amount of unnecessary extras; the systematic use of sales pressure, with arguments such as "everyone does it like this"; and not least the bizarre tradition of having virtually all corpses embalmed (even those that are to be cremated), a practice that is both costly and harmful to the environment.

Embalming is supposed to provide mourners with a way of saying goodbye to the deceased in an open coffin without having to deal too much with death's physical consequences. The modern practice of embalming can be traced back to the American Civil War, when a new method of preserving corpses was tested and improved upon on the battlefield. Profit-seeking amateur embalmers set up tents on the edge of the fray, where they pumped arsenic and mercury into the bodies of fallen soldiers, so that they could be sent by train without decomposing on the hot journey north. This gave families who could afford it the opportunity to say their final farewells and bury their sons as they wished. Although the results of the treatment were for a long time quite unpredictable, and the technique was far from perfect, as many as 40,000 of the 600,000 who fell during the war were treated using this early form of chemical embalming. But what really boosted the practice, turning it slowly but surely into a quite normal part of the professional funeral industry in the United States, was the death of Abraham Lincoln, and his funeral procession that went round the country in 1865, just after the Civil War. For three weeks, the coffin containing the embalmed president traveled by train from city to city, all the way back to Springfield, Illinois, where he was finally buried in Oak Ridge Cemetery. During this journey, people could honor the late president, mourn, and pay their respects beside the open casket in which Lincoln lay, looking at first very lifelike, but as the weeks went by, more and more like a "ghastly shadow" of himself.

THE PROFESSIONALIZATION AND commercialization that occurred in many industries during the industrialization of the 1800s is often linked to the raw and untamed market liberalism that principally impacted those who were already the most deprived. So the fact that the funeral industry followed in a similar vein might not come as a surprise. Nevertheless, the scale of the funeral industry's profit-seeking and deception seemed appalling to the well-read middle class in 1963. It gave the business an image problem that it continues to struggle with today, and prompted a countercultural search for alternatives, often referred to as the "alternative death movement," which we will return to in later chapters.

During the eighteenth and nineteenth centuries, professionalization took place in another, somewhat related, sector. Developments within the field of medicine advanced rapidly, and the process of educating future doctors helped to further our knowledge about the body's interior. The goal was to acquire a greater understanding of the human body in order to increase people's life expectancy and prevent death, in addition to fighting diseases and ailments during life. Central to both the research and the training was anatomy teaching. And this new branch of medicine, the standard-bearer of rationality, required a constant supply of human bodies for dissection.

Today, when a dead body is donated for research, it is embalmed within a few days of death (using far better methods than in the mid-1800s). This means that the body can be preserved for up to three years and used for teaching by doctors, specialists, and other healthcare professionals. Students will often work with the same body over a long period of time. In Great Britain, around 1,300 bodies are donated to science every year; in the United States, the number is around 20,000.

At the start of the 1800s, the practice of organ donation had not yet started. The only way educational institutions could acquire corpses for dissection, legally, would be to use the bodies of criminals who had been sentenced to death and executed. This was particularly true in Great Britain and the United States, where the law did not allow the bodies of individuals who had died in jails, poorhouses, orphanages, or other forms of public institutions to be delivered to the anatomy rooms as they did in several other European countries. Dissection was often seen as a form of punishment in itself, and it could not be authorized without being in connection with a sentence.

During this self-proclaimed "era of progress," however, sentencing criminals to death for less serious crimes became less common. As a consequence, doctors and medical students faced a constant shortage of dead bodies. The solution they found involved entering into a kind of informal collaboration with another "profession" that saw the light of day, or more aptly the darkness of night, around the turn of the eighteenth century.

GRAVE ROBBERS HAVE probably been around as long as graves. When archaeologists examine burial mounds or other burial structures it is relatively common to find that others have been there already. Sometimes it will have been shortly after the actual burial, other times hundreds or even thousands of years later. Some might even claim that archaeologists are not just in the business of death but are (to a certain extent, academically rarefied) grave robbers themselves! Think of all the tombs that have been opened, their contents shipped off to research institutions and museums in nearby and faraway countries. Fortunately, in most countries, professional archaeology is now regulated to prevent the destruction of cultural heritage. It is worth mentioning, however, that following the rise of scientific interest in Egyptian antiquities—something which is often linked to Napoleon's military expedition in 1798—the scope of the black market also expanded considerably. Throughout the 1800s, while Egyptology and archaeology developed as scientific disciplines, museums and private collections in Europe and America were filled with incredible treasures taken from the graves of Egyptian kings and priests. But it was not just the scientists who were interested in what they (or their local workers) found. When the authorities eventually began regulating the sale and export of Egypt's cultural heritage, the black market became even more attractive to foreign buyers. To this day, we constantly see the ripple effects of this problematic interaction between grave robbers, academics, more-or-less legitimate traders of antiquities, and wealthy collectors, especially within weak nation-states or areas plagued by recurring armed conflict.

Today we find slivers of Egypt's rich past in museums all over the world—not only artifacts, monuments, and papyri scrolls but the famously mummified human remains of elite individuals, mentioned here because they also represent another business of death, dating back thousands of years. The ancient Egyptians prac-ticed deliberate mummification as early as 2,500 BCE, but the most well-preserved mummies date back to a period 1,000 to 1,500 years later. Initially this was a very expensive practice, afforded only to pharaohs and priests, but eventually being mummified after death became more common: any Egyptian that could afford it, could have it. A specific group of priests were responsible for and made a living from embalming. The process lasted seventy days and took place in small purpose-built workshops. Other than what we have learned from the mummies themselves, the methods best known to us are described by the Greek historian Herodotus, who traveled to Egypt around 450 BCE.

Depending on the price one was willing to pay, mummification varied in quality and method. One of several mummies who have been studied over the last decades through modern X-rays and CT scans is "Nofret": a particularly well-preserved mummy of a middle-aged woman that was gifted to the Cultural History Museum in Oslo by King Oscar II in 1889. Her treatment after death exem-plifies the professionalism of many ancient Egyptian embalmers. All of Nofret's internal organs had been removed from the body, except for the heart, which, after being salted and bandaged, had been returned to her chest. The other organs were put in small jars to be placed in the tomb alongside the mummified body. Her brain would have been pulled out through the nose using hooks before her body was covered in salt, to remove all the moisture. Once the body was totally desiccated, Nofret was oiled and bandaged, finger by finger, body part by body part, but first both her abdomen and skull were partially filled with fragrant antiseptic resin. The band-ages were then covered with viscous bitumen, or a kind of "natural asphalt." The treatment ensured the physical preservation of the body for eternity, and thus, eternal life. The X-rays and CT scans carried out in 2002, about 2,200 years after she was buried, show that the skeleton is so well preserved that the images could be of someone living today.

Nevertheless, Nofret's mummified remains probably would not have been much use in an anatomical dissection. The grave robbers operating in England around the same time as the Egyptologists, who began helping themselves to what was in Egypt's burial chambers, only wanted *fresh* corpses. Any other grave goods they found were left behind: if you were caught with jewelry or clothes that had been placed in a grave you risked a long prison sentence, but no one "owned" a corpse itself, so body snatching existed in a kind of legal blind spot.

It obviously went against the morals and decency of ordinary people, but precisely how it was forbidden, and on whose authority, was quite unclear. Those arrested for stealing corpses were often given only a mild reprimand—a day or two behind bars, perhaps—before they were released and free to continue their often lucrative trade. There are many sources referring to the pricing and negotiations over a dead person's value. The price would be affected by whether it was a man or a woman, whether they were old or young, in good or not-so-good condition, and so on. One of London's body snatchers even kept a diary for a short while between 1811 and 1812. The account of each day usually finished with "everyone got drunk."

The supply of corpses usually came from disheveled men, petty crooks, and other dubious types; people who existed on the fringes of society. But the demand was driven by civilized society's medical profession, and its students. In the United States there were several large riots between 1765 and 1854, where doctors and students were chased by furious mobs enraged about the desecration of the dead and how you could not be sure that your loved ones would rest in peace after burial. In 1788, doctors at the New York Hospital had to seek refuge in the prison, behind bars, to avoid the 5,000 demonstrators who stood outside shouting "Bring out your doctors!" Twenty people were said to have died in the chaos. Following similar riots, the University of Maryland in Baltimore built an underground corridor from the anatomy hall in case evacuation became necessary. But the corridor was not just a practical escape route; it was used by the school's own janitor and body snatcher—or "resurrectionist," as the grave robbers often were called—to transport corpses back and forth to the lecture hall.

The robbers developed their own methods to ensure fast and efficient delivery. They chose primarily to loot pauper's graves—and in the United States the burial grounds of African Americans, since it caused less outrage and controversy. When the upper classes became victims of grave robbing, there would often be trouble. The New York riot was triggered by a mere rumor that the body of a young, unnamed middle-class woman had been seen in a dissection room several days after her funeral. Grave robbers often worked together in a network of scouts, lookouts, diggers, cart drivers, and middlemen connected to the buyers, who would usually split the profit between them based on pre-agreed rates. Normally they would observe a funeral during the day, noting the coffin's position, then return under the cover of darkness and make a precise cut into the coffin's head. Hooks were then placed under the arms of the corpse, or around its neck, and the body pulled out, before neatly returning the soil to the grave so as to leave it looking untouched.

If they were lucky, no one would notice the robbery. What you don't know, can't hurt you.

Hospitals in Baltimore were early leaders in medical research, and, parallel to this, an efficient and professional body-snatching network emerged, which made the city a focal point for the buying and selling of cadavers. When a rail connection was established in 1828, reliable transport to other major cities whose universities and hospitals also needed bodies for the anatomy rooms greatly expanded the business. Baltimore's climate helped, too, because, unlike the big cities of the north, such as Boston, it was rarely cold enough to freeze the soil, so in the winter months especially many corpses were transported north. As a means of hiding the cargo while also preventing it from smelling en route, the bodies would sometimes be stuffed into barrels of whiskey. This did not go to waste either: the liquor was sold as "stiff drink" or "rotgut."

In London, a pub called the Fortune of War became a notorious meeting point for body snatchers. It is said that exhumed corpses would even be stacked behind the bar, awaiting delivery. In Sarah Wise's book *The Italian Boy: Murder and Grave-Robbery in 1830s London*, among the testimonies, old newspaper articles, and court documents, we learn how those with bodies to convey often ran back and forth between buyers: how they negotiated prices, were outbid by other bidders, retrieved corpses that were no longer needed, and so on. Since doctors were not interested in teeth, the grave robbers—who were interested in maximizing profit—would extract nice specimens from a corpse's jaws and sell them on to dentists and denture makers.

In all its gruesomeness, it was pretty much like any other petty trade where finding smart ways of maximizing profit meant the difference between just getting by and, at best, making a killing. Like fishmongers, success for a corpse-monger depended on finding the freshest body possible. Fed up with his suppliers, Baltimore doctor Randolph Winslow took matters into his own hands and began stealing corpses himself. When he was found out, it was a minor scandal, although it did not cause any serious harm to his career; he later became head of the American Surgical Association and the Baltimore Medical Association.

The constant hunt for nice, fresh corpses led some body snatchers to go even further. In November 1831, the body of a boy aged about fourteen was delivered to King's College, London, prompting a reaction from the surgeon in charge of the dissection, Richard Partridge. The body appeared "suspiciously fresh," it did not seem like the boy had been buried, and death appeared to have been caused by a heavy blow to the back of his head. Partridge tricked the men who delivered the body into waiting there, while he notified the police.

The men, John Bishop and Thomas Williams, members of a notorious gang of "resurrectionists," were convicted of this and several other premeditated murders. They were eventually hanged before a crowd of onlookers. As an extra punishment, they were dissected in the same anatomy rooms they had for years supplied cadavers to. Before his execution, Bishop admitted that over a period of twelve years he had exhumed somewhere between five hundred and a thousand bodies. Following this and several other well-publicized cases of murders committed by body-snatchers William Burke and William Hare were convicted in Edinburgh around the same time of sixteen murders related to the sale of corpses for dissection—the laws in Great Britain were finally changed. In 1832, the Anatomy Act permitted several legal ways of obtaining corpses, which meant that the illegal trading of bodies gradually disappeared, although in the United States it continued until the end of the century when various state laws finally put an end to the practice.

TODAY'S DEATH PROFESSIONS use a lot of energy on their relationship with the living and see it as their duty to maintain the dignity of the dead. The procedures surrounding today's dissections are formalized through strict ethical guidelines, which are further reinforced by the professional environment through non-statutory practices. Some places even hold memorial services, for people who have chosen to donate their bodies to science, where the relatives, the students who carried out the dissection, and university staff will pay their respects when what's left of the deceased is finally buried or cremated. In her book *All That Remains: A Life in Death*, Susan Black, a professor of anatomy and forensic medicine, talks about an unusual but touching episode where, after much doubt and reflection, she allowed one of their future donors to witness a dissection similar to the one he himself was to undergo following his own death. All those involved had consented prior to their visit to the anatomy room, and the encounter between students and donor was seen as meaningful for all parties. The elderly man could put questions to the future doctors, and the students, in turn, could point, explain, and ask the curious dying man questions of their own.

Similar moves towards increased openness are happening in the funeral industry, in various degrees from place to place but nearly all beginning at smaller independent funeral homes, then spreading to the bigger and more commercial businesses. While the pricing and what went on in the back room were once shrouded in mystery, today's funeral homes are becoming more open, and "price transparency" is gradually becoming an industry standard. It is easy to see how much a coffin, urn, or headstone costs. The prices of various "all-inclusive" funeral packages are listed online. In many cities, funeral homes have even started offering competitive prices.

One thing that struck us during our conversations with funeral directors—considering how difficult it can be getting into a business where newcomers and competitors are not particularly encouraged—is how open they all are; how happily they answer our various questions, not just about prices but about the other aspects of their work, even practical things such as the plugging of orifices before the corpse is placed in the coffin. The consultants willingly talk about their preferred ways of looking after the dead: the corpse should be made up so much that it looks better, you should try to hide any contusions that might lead to the skin turning a bluish-purple color and cover up any injuries. Having said that, most of the people we spoke to insisted that you should never attempt to do so much that the deceased ends up looking "almost alive." "Our task is to look after the living and the dead, not to blur the boundaries between the two," said one.

Even problems and mistakes are discussed with surprising frankness. These can include funerals that went totally wrong, overly long eulogies that caused a queue outside the chapel, or hearses that got held up in the traffic. Funeral director Freddy Hultgren, our neighbor on the other side of the cemetery, recounted a time that he forgot to leave the box of soil to be thrown by the priest on the coffin ready, beside the coffin—a part of the ritual that is performed inside the chapel. Correcting the mistake while the priest spoke was impossible without the 150 relatives gathered in the church noticing. The solution was to improvise: "I stood in the aisle in clear view of the priest, who acknowledged that he'd seen me. I knew exactly which point in the ceremony the soil-throwing was due. When the time came, I walked down the aisle with the box and presented it to the priest. It then became a nice moment instead of a problem. The family thought it was nicely done."

5

Choosing a Coffin

Among the Nupe people of Nigeria, it is said that God created death because people had started carrying around wooden logs, burying them, and mourning them. So, according to this legend, the coffin, mourning, and funeral existed before death itself. The connection in modern Western tradition is probably not quite so causal. Nevertheless, the coffin is such a central element of a funeral that we can hardly imagine one without it. Even when a person dies and the body is never found, after a drowning accident, for example, memorial services will sometimes be held using an empty coffin. But it is never the other way round—never a corpse without a coffin.

The coffin's importance is even ratified by law in many countries. Section 29 of the Norwegian cemetery regulations specifies a number of requirements that should be met for a coffin to be legally used for standard burials. As previously mentioned, the coffin must be built from a material that will break down in the soil within a few years. If nobody wants to fix or continue the "lease" of the grave when the interment period expires, the grave will be reused. So it is of course essential for the coffin, and the corpse, to have become soil. The coffin must also be burnable in a cremation oven without emitting harmful gases, and "[it] must ignite no sooner than 10 seconds after being placed in a cremation oven, at a temperature of $1300°F$ ($700°C$)." The coffin must be made of wood. It must be no longer than 90 inches (230 cm); no wider than 31 inches (78 cm), including handles; and no higher than 23 inches (60 cm), including the feet, which should be at least four in number and 2 inches (5 cm) high. The lid must be rounded and removable, and it must be able to withstand "the load of one man," that is, 1100 newtons— which means 271 pounds (122 kg)—distributed over a 12 x 4 inch (30 x 10 cm) area. The bottom of the coffin must be waterproof, and must not produce more than a liter of uncompressed ash.

Modern coffins are designed with a unique and invisible double feature. During the ceremony, the entire coffin, including the lid, must be able to withstand the weight of a man, because in the event of the coffin overturning, you would not want the corpse rolling out. But when the coffin is safely in the ground, it is also important for the lid to give way first. So the coffin lid has a built-in weakness, which *allows* it to eventually collapse. In anticipation of this, new graves are topped with a heap of soil called a "positive soil mound." This makes a recently filled grave stick up like a tiny mountain range. It highlights the fact that the deceased is only recently buried and has not yet settled. Then, after a few weeks, you can see that the soil above the grave has become level with the ground; this means that the lid has given way. The coffin will be full of soil, and the decomposition of the corpse is well underway.

All of the graves in the graveyard around our house contain either a coffin or an urn. Muslims, and a number of other, smaller religious communities, have a general rule that a corpse must be swaddled and placed in the grave as it is, without a coffin. So government requirements in countries like Norway, which enforce the use of coffins, were long considered to be a violation of the Muslim community's right to free religious practice. For decades, efforts were made to get special exemptions for religious minorities, and during a government review in 2008, it was decided that the laws regarding cemeteries, cremation, and funerals should be amended. In 2012, a new law was passed which stated that "burials should be conducted in a manner respectful to the deceased's religion or way of life," so from then on cemetery authorities could grant permission for burials that did not use coffins.

This was seen as a major victory for Norway's Muslim minority. Within Muslim burial customs, there are two main traditions. One of them—Al-Shaq—involves the digging of a vertical grave, which is quite similar to a standard grave except that it has two levels, one where those who have to inter the corpse should stand, and another level, slightly higher, where the corpse will lie. The corpse is then covered with planks or a large sheet of wood before the grave is filled without the soil coming into direct contact with the corpse. The other tradition—Al-Lahed—also features a vertical grave, but it has a horizontal niche beside it where the corpse will lie, so that again, when the soil is thrown in, none of it lands directly on the corpse.

These are traditions that have developed in countries further south. In most Middle Eastern countries, the ground is dry and compact, more sand than soil. In more northerly countries—not just ones in the far north like Norway, but most of those in central and northern Europe and the United States—the soil is heavier, wetter, and more plastic. It collapses a lot more easily, and water often seeps into the bottom of the grave. In many traditionally Christian countries in the north, Muslim graveyards have developed entirely new systems to make traditional Muslim burials possible, using special scaffolding to prevent graves from collapsing during the ceremony. In Norway, the Muslim communities that fought for exemptions from the culturally and religiously insensitive regulations, and won, appreciated their victory, but went on to adopt the same practice as the majority of the population. Coffins are seen as a part of national tradition, born as much out of natural conditions as they are of any specific religion. What is crucial is preventing the soil from touching the corpse, and a coffin, particularly a coffin lid, serves that purpose.

When a baby is born, what a parent wants to hear the midwife say is that the child is "normal"—healthy and strong, just like any other child. Later, when we go to school and have careers, we tend to strive for excellence and exceptionalism. Then, in death, most people want to be shrouded in normality again. While traditions may vary from country to country or between particular groups of a population, there seem to be strong conventions about what constitutes a "normal" coffin—rules which most people adhere to. In Norway coffins painted white were such an integral part of the funeral that right up until the 2000s, it was rare for mourners to be offered any alternatives.

"We just used to say that 'we assume you want the usual white coffin,'" explains Gunnar Hammersmark, a person who entered the business in 1969 and is today the director of the trade organization for the Norwegian funeral industry. The funeral home and the funeral consultant saw it as their job to read the audience and tailor their offer to what they assumed the customer would want. If the customer was obviously wealthy, that person would be given the chance to buy a more expensive model. "Or perhaps you'd like something a little more ornate, in cherrywood," the funeral consultant might suggest. Customers with a clearly strained budget, however, would be informed about simpler models. The purchasing situation was opaque and the options unclear: only the most persistent customer would ask to see the catalogue showing all the different models. The choice was primarily up to the funeral home, who, depending on their own discretion and decency, could control what the customer selected.

In *The American Way of Death*, Mitford explains how the American procedure for selling a coffin followed an intricate and devious pattern. Considering that the average price of a coffin was $400, the funeral home obviously wanted to sell a more expensive version. But how could this be done without simultaneously appearing greedy? The funeral consultant that Mitford describes is a salesman who pretends he is not a salesman. He is only there to channel the wishes and needs of the bereaved—and by doing so protect the dignity of the deceased and the solemnity of the event.

When it came to the sale of coffins, this would be done by giving the bereaved a sense of having full control. Instead of pointing out "the usual white coffin," the funeral consultant would allow the bereaved to view the different models. These coffins were to be placed randomly around the room. Under no circumstances should they be displayed in ascending or descending order of price, and it was important that the most expensive models were not placed too low down or at the back.

If the bereaved selected a coffin that was above the average price, it was their choice. "A very good choice, madam, a beautiful coffin." If they pointed out one that was cheaper, the task was simply to offer a response that led to more questions. "Yes, that's nice too. A very *simple* design," would invariably lead to a demand to see more options. If the customer pointed out a $400 coffin, they would usually ask to see another model as well. The funeral director would then respond, in accordance with the usual sales practice, by pointing out a coffin valued at $560. Sometimes the bereaved would immediately choose the more expensive model, which in this case would be a significant up-sell, 40 percent more than the average price. In other cases, the customer might be appalled by the cost and ask to be shown a cheaper model. The funeral consultant would then point out one of the cheapest coffins, perhaps a model for $280 or $320. This was nearly always a simple-looking coffin with no fittings, made from a visibly coarser material. For most customers, this option would be far from what they wanted. Their request to see something more affordable may have stemmed from their being unable to pay more, or because they simply did not *want* to pay more. But what they did not want, under any circumstances, was for all of the other mourners to see that they had chosen a cheap model. A tacky, *unworthy* model. So after being presented with the cheapest model, they would probably ask to see another alternative, at which point the funeral consultant would show them one costing $480. A compromise of sorts, but still 20 percent more expensive than the average model.

As with so many practices stemming from American culture and business, many of the things described by Mitford in 1963 have spread to other countries, particularly in Europe and Canada. In the 1990s Norway's largest chain of funeral homes, Jølstad, was bought by Service Corporation International. SCI was America's leading death-care company and had almost 4,000 funeral homes, five hundred privately run cemeteries, and two hundred crematoriums throughout the United States and twenty other countries.

One of the first things the Americans did was to change the sales situation. Normally the largest and nicest room at the funeral home would be used as a meeting and conference room, sometimes as a staff room. But the American owners said that these rooms should be turned into sales rooms for the coffins—although they were careful not to call them that. Instead, they were called "showrooms," where the coffins would be displayed so that the bereaved could see them for themselves.

Instead of adopting the full-blown and rather cynical American sales strategy for up-selling described by Mitford, the staff often chose to leave the room when the bereaved viewed the coffins. "We're probably more discreet in Norway," explains Hammersmark, who was a company employee at the time of the American takeover.

Faced with so many alternatives, customers nevertheless ended up choosing differently to how they chose in the past. The most popular model was still the standard white coffin; a few chose a cheaper one, but far more than previously ended up choosing more expensive coffins. "We saw it in our net income. We were making more money from the coffins," says Hammersmark. "And at the same time, our customers were more satisfied. They felt they had made a more personal choice, which suited them."

In 2000, the American company sold its Norwegian and many of its other foreign stakes, after misguided investments and large debts caused the share price on the Dow Jones to fall from $43 to less than $2. But the new tradition within coffin sales remained. Today, most funeral homes have a separate coffin room where the bereaved can view the coffins and see the craftsmanship and details—which largely determine the price—for themselves.

Freddy Hultgren's coffin room at Aker Funeral Directors is right beside the reception room. Coffins take up a lot of space, so instead of whole coffins, only the end sections are displayed. This allows customers to check the detailing on the various models, to see and feel the difference in textures and fittings, without the room being crowded. As well as coffins, a number of urns are on display. Hultgren says that he supports transparency around the prices, just as he is open about other aspects of the process. He does not want to hide the fact that the various parts of a funeral are expensive, which is why he chooses to display the price beside all the coffins and urns.

A coffin is not a utility item in the normal sense. The person using it gets no specific pleasure from its design or detailing, and the bereaved have minimal contact with it. In the church, chapel, or ceremony room it will stand there for an hour or two, barely visible since it will often be covered with flowers. The only time a coffin is visible to all those present is when it is being carried out after the ceremony, and even then only for a few short minutes.

In some cases, nobody will see the coffin. Some families choose to forego the actual funeral service and instead hold a memorial or urn-interment ceremony afterwards. In those cases, the deceased is collected, placed in the coffin, and transported—via a cold room—to the crematorium, where the coffin and body are burned with nobody but the employees of the funeral home and the crematorium having seen them. In some cases, the deceased will have no mourners; in other cases, there will only be relatives who want nothing to do with the funeral. Nevertheless, everyone has to have a coffin.

The alternatives are few and far between. In Norway there is a long tradition of "doing it yourself," typified by so many endless renovation projects on cabins and houses, and cars in the garage. In 2017, the designer Bård Løtveit joined forces with the furniture manufacturer Aanesland and launched *Norgeskisten*, a DIY coffin made from Norwegian spruce that comes as a building kit, flat-packed like a piece of IKEA furniture. The idea is that the bereaved will have a shared experience of building and perhaps even decorating the coffin. It was shown at a number of fairs and exhibitions and received a huge amount of attention when it was launched, although so far sales have been modest.

The vast majority of people choose to buy ready-made coffins, and these are marketed in a language that is both evocative and opaque: "Watercolor 15" is a black lacquered coffin, with a hinged lid. "It is upholstered in cotton fabric, and delivered with a mattress, blanket, and pillow." The manufacturer's price is $430, excluding tax, and it is considered a "standard model": neither particularly nice nor tacky, and costing around $1,450 when bought from the funeral home.

"Lilje," which comes in solid, white-painted pine, with no decoration, costs $1,200, including VAT, while Lilje with a high-gloss finish costs $1,430. These are the successors to the standard white coffin. Most of the models displayed in the viewing room at Aker Funeral Directors cost between $1,140 and $1,860. The most expensive models, displayed on the neighboring wall in oak and cherrywood, cost between $2,700 and $4,660.

The really exclusive models stand out clearly. They look bigger and shinier, like a limousine among family cars. The emphasis here is on details. While an expensive car has more legroom, the "Continental 50" has a full 20 inches (51 cm) height under the lid, almost 4 inches (10 cm) more than most of the others. This is a "classic coffin of the highest quality in mahogany-stained cherrywood and with a high-gloss surface. The coffin is equipped with a split lid, a strong plinth, and a cherrywood handle. A very exclusive model in a high price range." Most funeral homes list this coffin at over $4,660.

These coffins are not only significantly more expensive. Since oak and other hardwoods take longer to decompose, the standard twenty-year interment period is not sufficient. Instead, you have to pay for what's called "eternal interment." This currently costs $2,500, which is a significant additional expense, even if the annual fee does become negligible if you divide it by infinity.

Scandinavian oak coffins have in fact been linked to eternity since ancient times. They are some of the very oldest coffins we know of anywhere in the world. Between 1500 and 1100 BCE, many people were buried in coffins made of hollowed-out oak trunks, which were placed in huge mounds that have stood as powerful monuments in the Danish landscape until recent times. These mounds were made of turf lain with the grass-side down, which led to the mound's interior effectively retaining moisture. Over the centuries and millennia, a chemical process in the soil created an iron-rich layer of earth called "hardpan," which smothered the oak coffins. Since oak already lasts longer in soil than other types of wood, this hardpan ensured that the oak coffins—often including the deceased themselves and the objects with which they were buried—were preserved more or less intact until many of the mounds were removed in the late 1800s and early 1900s.

At the National Museum of Denmark, you can now peer, with the aid of subdued lighting, into the graves of some of these Bronze Age people, the best known of whom is the Egtved Girl, who died between sixteen and eighteen years old, probably in the late summer of 1370 BCE.

Egtved Girl's coffin is a debarked and hollowed-out oak trunk that was split in two. The growth rings in the trunk allow scientists to determine the grave's exact age. The top part of the trunk, which once served as a lid, now hangs precariously above the heads of those who lean over the edge of the coffin for a closer look at the imprint of the girl, which is still visible. Apart from some hair and teeth, there is not much left of Egtved Girl's earthly remains; her bones have crumbled due to the conditions in the coffin. Her clothes, however, like many of those found in other oak coffins, are incredibly well preserved. She was buried wearing a short jersey made of finely woven wool, a knee-length string skirt, and a large bronze belt-plate featuring a circular decoration reminiscent of the sun, which is typical of the period. We can see that the girl was carefully placed in the coffin, on a bed of soft cowhide. She had a wide woolen blanket spread over her, quite similar to how we arrange a coffin for our dead today. Egtved Girl took other things to her grave, too, such as a bucket containing traces of beer. Drinking beer as part of a funeral rite, or to commemorate the deceased, is something most northerners can identify with. What is more difficult for us to understand, perhaps, is the bundle of cremated bones of a child that was placed with her. Why would a young girl be buried with remains of another child who had received dramatically different treatment after death?

Recent analysis of Egtved Girl's hair and teeth has shown that she was not buried among the people she had grown up with. On the contrary, she had come from the south, somewhere in Germany, and had most likely been back there just a short time before she died. The child lying at the foot of the coffin was five or six years old when they died. The age difference between the child and the Egtved Girl was no more than ten to twelve years, so we can imagine the child being the girl's brother or sister. Perhaps the younger child died on the long journey, and perhaps that is why the body was burned—because it had to be transported? Perhaps Egtved Girl also fell ill on the same journey, and perhaps that explains why she died at such a young age? Was the child a beloved brother or sister, or a necessary sacrifice?

The story of Egtved Girl's life and death, along with the remains of other oak-coffin burials from the same period, have provided us with lots of information not just about death and burials but about life in the Bronze Age. We know, for example, that some

individuals traveled long distances. We know about their clothing and elaborate hairstyles. We also know that certain people
had positions in society that warranted their interment in a burial
mound—something that required hundreds of working hours, and
not least massive amounts of topsoil that was utilized in the construction. In other words, those we have learnt about, from beyond
the grave, must have been the elite of the Nordic Bronze Age. Just
as the oak coffins at today's funeral homes are reserved for the
well-heeled, it is also obvious that 3,500 years ago oak coffins were
only available to the very wealthiest.

Today, the most important thing about selling coffins to a
modern customer-mourner is that it should look like a necessity,
not an acquisition. The practice, in our part of the world, which
states that the deceased should be placed in coffins on their way
to the oven or the soil, is a part of a heavily regulated system,
and is no longer one of the individual choices we allow ourselves
to make when facing death. It is a cultural practice, preferred
by the majority, which has ultimately been legislated, making it
practical for the industry that helps us manage death. Perhaps
that is why coffins are so alike, in the market economy's name of
decency, with just a subtle hint of prestige for some of the more
expensive models.

IN OTHER PARTS of the world, the coffin selection process
is a far cry from "the standard white." When we heard that our
friend Emerson Skeens in Zanzibar was terminally ill, and that
he didn't have long, we flew down to visit him and say goodbye.
On our arrival, we went straight from the airport to the house on
Sokomohogo Street—a narrow alley among the labyrinth of winding lanes in Zanzibar's capital, Stone Town—where Emerson had a

top floor apartment with a large bedroom, a desk, and a traditional four-poster Zanzibar bed.

Emerson was lying in bed. In his prime he had been a powerful, muscular man who loved bodybuilding, both as a vanity project and as a way of connecting with young men who used the gym equipment in his back garden. In the months that had passed since the cancer had struck, he had gone from looking buff and younger than his sixty years to being a hollow-cheeked, gaunt older man, with almost transparent skin and ugly sores on his calves. He was bare-chested and had a kanga tied round his waist.

"I can't stay awake very long now without having to rest a bit," he said after welcoming us in. Then he dozed off.

He was woken again by the housekeeper, who knocked on the door frame and said that another visitor had arrived. Emerson pushed himself up in bed, noticeably perkier after a little sleep.

"I just have to talk with the fundi," he said apologetically.

A large man in a blue T-shirt walked in, and after exchanging pleasantries the two men started looking at a little red notebook full of sketches. The meeting followed the usual rhythm of a Zanzibarian business meeting, first cautiously and respectfully, then eventually, as they began discussing prices, loudly and energetically.

It was possible to catch some of the expressions in Swahili, things like "You must be crazy," and "That's way too expensive!"

When the meeting ran over time, Emerson apologized again. "Sorry for the delay, but Suleyman is the fundi who's making my coffin, so we have to try and settle this now."

They discussed the various types of wood: some were problematic to use since they were not fully dried out and would make the coffin difficult to paint. After a while another guy dropped by so that Emerson could decide on the flowers he wanted. He chose some beautiful purple ones similar to those framing his bedroom door, before sending the man on his way.

Emerson and Suleyman continued their negotiating, until eventually Emerson decided on a wood type and a design. The coffin had to be simple but elegant: not a lot of metal, but clean lines and quality wood. It should be comfortable to carry. They looked at a few decorative details before starting a final round of haggling.

"Don't try fooling me now," said Emerson. "No, of course not," Suleyman assured him before showing Emerson the calculation. Beneath the total, 668,000 shillings (roughly $250) he had written *Jumla*—meaning wholesale price. "That's because we are friends, Babu," he said, using the informal and affectionate term for grandfather. The meeting was then wound up with a few kind words, hugs, and assurances that the coffin would be finished in time.

Emerson was tired, but pleased that he'd got it over with. "I'm sure it will be a nice coffin," he said. "One well suited to me."

IN WESTERN, CHRISTIAN-DOMINATED and later humanist tradition it is said that we are all equal in death, and in Norway we say there are no pockets in the mortuary shirt—you can't take anything with you when you go. Perhaps the variations of the same coffin offered by our local funeral consultants are a reflection of ingrained Protestant restraint? The traditions are certainly more ostentatious further south in Europe. The funeral's place—as an important way of displaying social status, for reinforcing and creating identity, and confirming a person's belonging in the local community—is probably still the rule, not the exception, in most cultures. Small and large differences indicate both the deceased's and the bereaved family's standing.

Few places have seen a greater surge of interest in coffins than Ghana. The area around the capital, Accra, is famous for its elaborate and artfully designed coffins, which are as far from the "standard white" as you can imagine. In Ghana, there are coffins everywhere, like brightly colored memento mori, reminders that we are all going to die, and that when we do, we can choose to be buried in style. Funeral directors and coffin makers have their offices and workshops along the main roads for everyone to see. To make the coffins more visible, many even bring them out onto the pavement, forcing pedestrians, people out shopping or going to work, to walk around them.

Kudjoe Affutu is one of Ghana's—and thus the world's—most renowned coffin makers, an exponent of a type of functional artwork often referred to as "fantasy coffins." The tradition stems from the Ga people in the country's Accra region, whose chiefs would, on special occasions, be paraded around in figurative palanquins normally shaped like roosters or lions.

When a chief died, he would be buried in the same palanquin to commemorate the end of his reign. In some cases, a coffin would be produced based on the same symbol, or the existing palanquin would be converted into a coffin by having a lid attached to it. The son, or whoever took over the position, could use a different symbol, just as kings in modern monarchies will often choose their own motto. The palanquin, now a coffin, signified the chief's identity and position in death, just as the chair had done in life.

In the loft above Kudjoe's workshop there are rows of coffins, some finished, some works in progress; one shaped like a cobra, another like a crocodile. These coffins are being made for fetish priests—a type of sorcerer who offers various religious services, everything from curing impotence or providing marriage guidance to throwing curses or boosting your chances of winning the lottery.

"It's important for them to be feared, so they prefer coffins that symbolize frightening and deadly animals," explains Kudjoe.

In the loft there is also a coffin shaped like a pile of money, a coffin shaped like a beer can, and in the corner a smaller object, an urn, in the shape of an alien. "That's not for a funeral, it's a figure I made for a Swiss customer. I do art projects too, mostly abroad. A few years ago I was in Paris and exhibited at a place called the Pompidou Center. Do you know it? I made a coffin that was shaped like the center itself."

Ghanaian fantasy coffins are a mixture of utility object and artwork; in *The Buried Treasures of the Ga*, the Swiss social anthropologist Regula Tschumi writes about their origin. When the country's population grew rapidly after its liberation from British colonial rule in the 1950s, it coincided with a partial dissolution of the traditional tribal structures and their rules and restrictions. From then on, special coffins were no longer the sole entitlement of tribal chiefs; anyone with enough money could now have a special coffin made. And as a result, the motifs changed too.

Central in the development of coffins from local curiosities to internationally recognized art were a handful of coffin makers. Two of them, Kane Kwei and Paa Joe, were discovered by Western art historians and museum curators, and in 1989, an exhibition at the Musée d'art moderne in Paris gave them a major international breakthrough. This led to more international prestige, but it also spurred a creative explosion at home. There was a constant need to invent something new. The Ghanaian public, who had seen incredible coffins being sent to customers in Europe and the United States, began ordering similar models for their own dead.

Some of the coffins are hilariously funny; others are thought-provoking. Most of them are an expression of the person who will eventually lie in them. Among Paa Joe's most famous and eye-catching creations is a womb-coffin, originally made for a German gynecologist, and a replica of the Danish-Norwegian slave fort Christiansborg Castle—also known as the Gates of No Return. In Kane Kwei's workshop, near the center of Accra, we meet his son, Teshie Nungua, who shows off a Bible coffin that they are just finishing for a recently deceased priest, a coke bottle for a barman, a pile of folded clothes for a man who had a clothing stall at the market, and a sandal that was being made for the son of a chief. Nungua has already built his own coffin, shaped like a carpentry plane. "It's a symbol of my work," he explains.

Back at Kudjoe's workshop, Kwashi Jaboa's coffin is taking shape. Jaboa was an eighty-year-old cocoa farmer, and will be buried in a coffin resembling a cocoa bean; thicker in the middle and tapered at each end, with broad ridges along its length. Once the structure itself has been assembled using several pieces of carved wood, the work of plastering, sanding, and painting begins. The coffin's cocoa-bean shape emerges. In this dust-covered country—which does not have a single clean car and where every white wall has been kissed by a mixture of raindrops and red soil, in a landscape that looks pretty much like anywhere, with soda caps and three-legged stools scattered across the stony ground, and plastic bags blowing in the wind—the coffin's rough and lumpy shape is transformed into the most perfect and dazzling object imaginable. Neighbors and passers-by compliment Kudjoe on his work as he perfects the color pattern on the cocoa bean, then attaches a branch with two smaller cocoa beans to the side. A few hours later, the family arrives to collect the coffin. Jaboa's son, Jobi, invites us along to the ceremony.

Funerals are an important occasion in Ghana, an opportunity not just to say a last farewell to the deceased, but for the family to impress. And there is fierce competition. It's Saturday, and the traffic is extra bad since the road has suddenly been blocked by a large marquee. "What a Shock!" it says on the posters along the side. "Vida Dedei Thompson—Died Aged 41 Years." Two blocks down the road we run into a similar traffic jam, caused by preparations for the funeral of a Mrs. Comfort, and the celebration of "A Life Well Lived." We solve the problem by driving our car through an opening in the marquee. Religious fanatics who do not like the colorful and lively funerals that go far beyond the normal Christian tradition line the street, holding placards reminding people that "Hell Is Real—Turn to God Now!" The parties last for several days, and no expense is spared. "We're better at looking after the dead than the living," a frustrated Ghanaian told a BBC interviewer. When there is an election campaign, politicians will often pledge to introduce a four-day working week, to give people time to attend funerals.

For people used to funerals being something profoundly sorrowful, and deeply personal, the idea of attending the funeral of someone you never knew can seem a bit strange. But any reservations we have about imposing ourselves upon a grieving family vanish the moment we arrive. Hundreds of people are gathered in the square, where the commemoration has been going on since the day before. It starts with a partly frozen corpse at the Lit de Parade (the deceased had been in cold storage for two months while the coffin was being finished). When the coffin finally arrives, it is placed in the middle of the square among the orchestra and the dancing. Many of the attendees put money in a basket on top of the coffin—a collection that will help recover some of the family's expenses. People smile and laugh, sing, dance, and chatter. There's not a tear or an unhappy face to be seen.

After several hours of dancing and music, the coffin is lifted onto a truck. Some accompany it, but most stay behind. No one announces what's happening, or where they are going, but we catch up with the truck and the coffin at the gas station where the truck is getting its tires inflated. The coffin then makes the 8-mile (13 km) journey to the burial site accompanied by fifteen men stood on the truck's loading platform. The roads are disastrously bumpy: the men struggle to stay upright, and the cocoa-bean coffin with Kwashi Jaboa inside slides this way and that. The heat of the sun beats down, and when the truck hits a particularly large or sudden bump, the coffin lid bangs as if the person inside is trying to get out. The men standing beside it laugh.

Once at the gravesite, the coffin barely fits in the grave. It has to be stood on its end and pushed in, and the decorative branches with small cocoa beans have to be removed. Then the priest arrives. After singing a hymn, he pulls out a bottle of lily-scented deodorant and sprays it above the coffin, filling the air with the smell of a men's locker room. He then pulls out a box of talcum powder, which he sprinkles over the coffin.

"Here lies Kwashi Jaboa," he says. "And none of us know who will be next. So beware, and choose the path of righteousness." He casts a shovelful of soil onto the coffin, makes the sign of the cross, and then everyone returns to the party while the diggers refill the grave.

6

DUST TO DUST

Large sections of Oslo North Cemetery are formal and functional. The forty lots surrounding the chapel, and the twenty nearest the hospital, are flat and almost identical in shape and size—grids that are drawn up on paper first, and then later put into use, one by one. Nearest the chapel, where the oldest graves are situated, the headstones are quite varied. The cemetery authorities have chosen to continue maintaining some of the graves even after their maintenance periods expired.

Our cemetery lacks the abundance of formerly important people that the older, more centrally located cemeteries have—there's the odd poet, and a former government minister, but the graves here seem to have been selected mainly for aesthetic reasons; attempts at grandeur in otherwise modest surroundings. They pay tribute to long-forgotten ice traders, sheet-metal workers, tram conductors, army colonels, company directors, and even a few women, mostly defined by who their husbands were and honored as devoted wives.

As you move away from the chapel, the layout becomes increasingly monotonous. The postwar egalitarian mindset, which led to the endless rows of conformist tenements east of the cemetery, made people equal also in death—and here too there are square lots consisting of almost identical gray headstones and green grass, surrounded by gray gravel footpaths.

What prevents the entire cemetery becoming monotonous and alienating—what stops it from feeling like a mere grid system of death—is the landscaping. There are trees everywhere. And unlike the forest surrounding the city—which although hailed as giving the city a "closeness to nature" is basically just a giant spruce plantation—in the cemetery there is a unique variety of different species.

Parallel to the road there are birch trees with glowing white bark. And just inside the chapel's main road entrance, near the memorial to the communists who died in the Second World War, is a huge copper beech, its leaves bleeding over the living and the dead. In the large, open lot beside the hospital, the trunk of a pine tree has split near the top, giving it the appearance of a snake's forked tongue. In the spring, blossoming Japanese cherry trees compete with goat willows, and giant maples send their helicopter seeds whirling through the air like confetti. There is a row of cypresses that bend at the top as if bowing their heads in respect, while the conifers stand proudly: ugly and upright.

The cemetery is one of the most vibrant places in the city, more green, more beautiful, and more varied than most of its parks. Stein Olav Hohle, a former director of the municipal cemetery authority who started his career as one of their gardeners here in the 1970s, is an active member of the local conservation group Friends of the Trees and has arranged numerous tours of the place for those interested in learning more about the diverse nature there. He points out ash, elm, maple, larch, pine, flowering field maple, and crab apple trees. Sometimes he'll stop at a tree he planted decades ago, delighted at how tall it has grown, how beautiful it has become, concerned if it looks unhappy or if it has been damaged by an excavator.

AT SOME POINT in the late 1960s or early 1970s, the sunny little mound southwest of our house, with its elm and horse chestnut trees, started to be used for burials. It was one of the last areas to be absorbed into the gradual, hundred-year-long establishment of the cemetery. No attempt has been made to groom the landscape here, no effort to organize it in rows and groups. On the contrary, the graves fit round the topography, sunlight, and location of the trees. Instead of normal headstones, the graves are marked stones that seem to be naturally occurring. Round ones, square ones, and everything in between, half-buried in the ground—stones that could have been found in the surrounding countryside, or right there, with names and dates carved onto them. In some places the letters are covered in moss, so it's impossible to see who is resting below. A couple of benches sit discreetly in the middle of this lovely, quiet place, which feels almost like a forest.

This is part of a conscious development. In line with increasing urbanization and a growing population, it has become a stated policy that cemeteries—as well as fulfilling their main purpose as burial grounds—should also be nice places for the living, and that these green areas should play an important role in maintaining biodiversity. Many of the new generation of landscape gardeners working in cemeteries have backgrounds in organic farming. Instead of grooming cemeteries into ornamental gardens, they plant bee-friendly meadows that are never mowed, with perennials and other pollen-producing flowers. There are specific programs for composting, and plans are being made to leave dead trees where they are in order to provide insects with food. Many cemeteries have also installed bird boxes, insect hotels, and squirrel houses. When a cluster of sad-looking spruces east of our house were cut down, a few of them were stacked neatly and left to rot for the benefit of the local insects and microfauna. In Norway's oldest city, Tønsberg, entomologists recently reported that the rare and ungainly hermit beetle *Osmoderma eremita*, which had long been feared extinct, has survived in the cemetery's ancient ash trees.

In recent years, there has been a public turn towards nature—not just in our cemetery but in large parts of the Western world.

"I LOVE YOU, Grandma!" is written on a photo that shows two arms embracing not an old lady, but a tree. Another photo says, "Hi Dad!" beside a hand stroking the bark of an oak tree. In a third photo, "How you've grown, John!" beside what looks like the top of a conifer, possibly some kind of enormous pine, towering above. "These are our new postcard ads," explains Raoul Bretzel contentedly.

Bretzel is one of the designers of Capsula Mundi. Along with the Italian-Venezuelan designer Anna Citelli, he developed the model for a totally new way of burying people that was exhibited at the Salone del Mobile di Milano, or Milan Furniture Fair, in 2003. We met him at his workshop in Rome, a block away from Campo Verano, the city's largest cemetery. The workshop lies in a street full of small houses, most of which were, until recently, occupied by artisan companies like stonemasons and coffin makers, all providing services to the cemetery and the church. Most of these traditional craftsmen have now moved on, stepping aside for more modern companies, advertising agencies, and various consultancies. But several of the neighboring streets are still lined with funeral homes, and up towards the cemetery there is a flower market where competing traders will often use surprisingly aggressive and rowdy sales methods.

The debut at the Milan furniture show attracted a lot of international attention. Salone del Mobile is known for being the place where the world's top furniture designers get to shine, in a huge exhibition area comprising 26 buildings on the outskirts of the Italian fashion metropolis. At the 2003 show, there were over 2,200 exhibitors. The trend that year, according to the press, leant towards softer and more minimalist design. Light-colored wood was out, and there seemed to be a shift towards dark-stained oak and wenge brown. "The new style is warm, a response to the spirit of the times perhaps," mused a newspaper reporter who attended.

The show itself has often been criticized for being a trade fair dominated by large companies, rather than a showcase for innovation. In response, the organizers devoted space in the Salone Satellite pavilion to several younger designers. A designer from Vienna turned heads with his Snow Bench, a bench consisting of two specially designed snowboards, while an Australian design duo made their breakthrough with a polyethylene lamp that could be tilted from side to side without toppling over or breaking.

In the midst all this, many people stopped around an outlandish installation: a huge egg with a tree hanging over it. And they were no less perplexed when they learned what it was. A coffin. The egg was just big enough for an adult—a dead adult—to fit inside it in the fetal position.

The idea behind Capsula Mundi was to use design as a way of addressing the cultural taboo surrounding death. In modern Western culture we are concerned with looking strong and healthy, which makes talking about death, and the fact that we are all going to die, problematic. When we do relate to death, it is as something very sad, very dark—something we fear and keep out of sight.

"Death is only ever about loss. As designers, we wanted to use an object to create a different relationship to it," says Bretzel. Initially, he and Citelli knew little about the funeral industry. Their aim was to challenge the rigid framework set by the furniture show; a world concerned mainly with buying new, beautiful, and, to a greater or lesser extent, useful things. The information on their first brochure is philosophical and poetic: "The egg. A perfect shape, archaic, which has survived the passage of time . . . For all of us living beings, the egg is the universal symbol of life."

When their intended contribution to the Salone Satellite pavilion became known, there was a period of uncertainty as to whether they would be allowed to participate at all; the director of the show initially felt that their exhibit would not fit in. By the time they were finally accepted, they were very nervous. How would people react?

The capsule itself in Capsula Mundi, the egg, is in a way just a coffin made in a different shape and from a different material, consisting of soil and glue instead of wood. But what perhaps drew the most attention to the egg—apart from the fact that corpses were its intended target group—was the tree hanging above it.

It's a simple idea: The deceased's body is placed in an egg instead of a coffin. The egg—"the universal symbol of life"—is buried, much like a coffin, and a tree is planted on top. And this is where the whole concept gains a practical, organic purpose: As the tree grows, it draws its nourishment from the decomposing corpse. Death is thus able to give something back to life. It is beautiful and symbolic, a modern burial custom that has something timeless about it.

Capsula Mundi was not a scandal as the organizers had feared. Instead, it became one of the most talked-about objects. Whether the primary motivation at Capsula Mundi's launch in 2003 was a desire to create a piece of thought-provoking design bordering on art or to shake up the funeral sector is unclear, even after talking to Bretzel. But it does seem clear that the combination of praise and attention on the one hand and resistance on the other made it a project that the two designers refused to give up.

The cemetery as we know it, with its orderly rows and immutable stone memorials, would be transformed. Capsula Mundi's designers saw cemeteries eventually becoming like forests, and in that sense more similar to the beautiful tree-covered mound at our cemetery, where you can sit in the evening sun and feel like you are out in the countryside. But with Capsula Mundi, this idea took a large and important step further: a cemetery would no longer be a place of trees and headstones—that is, headstones serving their purpose as memorials, framed by borders of trees—but somewhere that the two elements are one, with the trees marking the graves and the graves giving life to the trees. Instead of tending the grave, a family can take care of the tree. And they are free to choose any tree they want, which turns the cemetery into an experience of diversity—a place with lots of different trees, and as a result different colors, smells, birds, and perhaps, eventually, other animals.

"We wanted to move away from the position of viewing death as sad, to what might be described as a more primordial view, from prehistoric times, where death is simply a part of life. When life ends, it is also the beginning of something else," Bretzel explains.

But it is a far broader vision than just creating a new type of cemetery where trees have replaced the headstones. As these trees grow, they will become a park or, ideally, a forest, a vibrant and dynamic green area. Some trees will reproduce, some will die. A lilac might stand there sulking, while an oak, a larch, or an olive tree grows tall and majestic. The result is life, quite simply.

The idea of a tree being a memorial to the dead is nothing new. Back in Zanzibar, on our way to visit the grave of our friend Emerson, we drove around some of the other cemeteries on the outskirts of Stone Town. The city has always been a place of change and expansion, with new residential areas being built on top of former graveyards several times.

"Since you never knew how long a grave would last, it was normal to plant a tree on top of it, preferably a big and beautiful one like a baobab or a jacaranda," explained an old friend of Emerson's who showed us around. He pointed out several large trees standing untouched among the chaotic jumble of new buildings. "It was such common practice we actually use it in an expression, a kind of friendly insult you can use during a quarrel—*I'll see you under the jacaranda tree.*"

Capsula Mundi has proved itself to be thought-provoking and groundbreaking. The two designers still get invited to participate in art exhibitions, debates, and academic symposia. But on its journey from provocative prototype to actually being used, the idea has encountered problems. It has been twenty years since the project's launch, and not one person has been buried in the capsule. Various laws—regulations about what sort of coffins are allowed—have presented formal obstacles.

Each country has its own rules, and in many countries these rules vary between provinces or states. Another, perhaps bigger, problem is space. In most of the world's densely populated areas, it is hard enough finding space for traditional cemeteries. Although a burial forest is an attractive concept, it is one with such a voracious appetite for space that few towns or cities—or sparsely populated rural areas where forests are timber—either can or want to prioritize one.

A smaller version of the project, using an urn instead of a coffin, has gone into production and been sold to a number of countries. The rules for spreading ashes and burying urns are far more liberal than those for coffin burials. Several countries allow urn burials with a tree planted on top in your own garden. At the same time, burying an urn full of ashes rather than a whole corpse partly defeats the revolutionizing purpose of Capsula Mundi, since the ashes of an urn provides no nourishment to the tree above it, and the practical and symbolic connection between tree, human body, and nature loses some of its power. The grand vision is reduced to a beautifully designed urn and a good story.

CAPSULA MUNDI IS one of the earliest examples of a small but increasingly significant trend: a desire for greener burials. As mentioned earlier, the commercialized funeral business in the USA has been criticized in recent decades, especially after the publication of Mitford's influential book. This criticism, however, does not just concern the economic aspects of funerals and the running of large, private cemeteries like they are golf courses for the dead. The very relationship between death and nature seems to have been displaced and distorted; the bereaved are reduced to consumers, and funeral homes see themselves as providers of a service—a player in the market, like everyone else. And since the industry has managed to convince its customers that embalming is part of the burial process, environmental pollution from embalmed corpses has also become a growing problem—a quite unnecessary, even counterproductive one at that, since the point of a burial is for the body to become soil.

As is often the case with large, commercially driven trends in the USA, countercultural criticism has not led to any significant change: the direction has been set, the process of commercial-ization has too much momentum, and there is too much at stake. The funeral industry is an economic force, with an annual national turnover of over $15 billion, even more if you count the adjacent industries. Large parts of the market are controlled by ten big companies, each of which has solid political connections.

But when the mainstream seems impossible to stop, smaller tributaries often form; in this case something called the "alterna-tive death movement," the term for a cluster of ecologically aware, communitarian, and very often new-age-inspired ideas and prac-tices. Much attention has been given to some solutions that at first glance—and sometimes at second, third, and fourth glance—seem more comical and far-fetched than genuinely practical. In recent years, the media have done stories about "death doulas" that help the dying cross over to the other side, whatever that might be; about "death cafes," where people meet, drink tea, and talk about death; and about "death parties" and "pre-funerals," where terminally ill people invite their friends to one last party where they can write a final message on the coffin which is placed in the middle of the room and tested by the host or hostess, dressed in a burial gown, as part of the festivities. In 2018, the creators of WeCroak gained success—and not least publicity—with their app which, for a fee, sent five daily reminders that death was coming, perhaps when you least expect it. It was marketed as an advanced form of mindfulness, supposedly inspired by a Bhutanese saying about how the only way to be happy is to contemplate death five times a day.

There is no reason to doubt that such eccentric ideas have the capacity to bring meaning and joy to their users, and not least much-needed work for hard-pressed feature journalists. But along-side these more gimmicky initiatives—sometimes in tandem with them, sometimes at real odds with them—a real movement has emerged, which has been working systematically to change established mortuary practices. This is particularly true on the West Coast of the USA.

Central to this work is funeral director Caitlin Doughty, who works in Los Angeles. Doughty is the founder of the Order of the Good Death, an association for people working in the funeral business along with academics and artists collectively working to change our relationship with death, burial, and mourning. In addition to the practical work and network building, she is an active blogger, a YouTuber with 1.5 million followers, and the author of three best-selling books with funny and quite self-explanatory titles like *Smoke Gets in Your Eyes and Other Lessons from the Crematory* (2014), *From Here to Eternity: Traveling the World to Find the Good Death* (2017), and the children's book *Will My Cat Eat My Eyeballs? Big Questions from Tiny Mortals about Death* (2019).

Someone else who has gained a lot of attention with a philosophical yet practical project is the American Korean artist Jae Rhim Lee, who in 2011 launched what she called an Infinity Death Suit; a black suit that looks like a cross between a ninja outfit and a skeleton costume. The suit also happens to be inset with living mushroom spores. The idea behind this, as Jae Rhim Lee explains in her TED Talk "My Mushroom Burial Suit," is for the fungal spores to help decompose the body and cleanse it of heavy metals, residual medicines, or any similar pollutants that might be left in the body. Lee has cultivated the right fungal spores by feeding them hair, dead skin cells, and "various body fluids." The suit is on sale via the company Coeio, and, unlike many of the measures that hope to change normal funeral practices, it does not require any special approval. In 2019—after the actor Luke Perry of *Beverly Hills 90210*

was buried in what has now been called the Infinity Burial Suit—
sales skyrocketed, and Coeio struggled to produce enough suits
that contain effective mushroom spores. The company has also
launched a similar suit for pets.

The most significant figure in this slightly anarchic movement
is probably Katrina Spade, who lives in Seattle, Washington. Spade
began working with mortuary practices as part of a master's degree
in architecture where she was studying the effects of traditional
burial and cremation on the environment. Why, she wondered—in
much the same way as Capsula Mundi founders Raoul Bretzel and
Anna Citelli—are we bound to a mortuary practice that is costly,
resource-intensive, and counteractive to the natural decomposition
process when, in reality, death is the most natural thing there is?

The result of Spade's master's thesis, which she delivered in
2013, was the design of a three-story silo that would function as a
composting system for human corpses. Bodies would be placed in
a room at the top of the construction, which confusingly resembles
a diving tower, along with wood chips and other organic material to
assist the decomposition. Thirty days later, it would be possible to
extract fully composted soil at the bottom. This composting tower
would process a whole series of human corpses simultaneously.
And much like a compost heap for garden waste or food scraps,
you would refill it when necessary.

TREATING LOVED ONES like household waste might seem like a
strange idea. Death is not an everyday event. A dead body, despite
being a problem in its immediate form, is not something we want
to dispose of as readily as other compostable material. And we can
assume that those who lived before us felt similarly. Graves—from
the ancient proto-graves in Atapuerca until the modern day—give

us some insight into how our ancestors handled death. But for every grave we find, there are countless others that have vanished. The majority of our ancestors never left any trace of themselves behind. Many graves will never be found because we do not dig where they were put. Even more will have simply disappeared gradually over time, returning to the earth's natural cycle. The older the grave, the more unlikely it is that there will be anything left of it, and how much is left depends on the preservation conditions. From the Early Stone Age—the period following the arrival of the first people in Scandinavia at the end of the last Ice Age—there are relatively few known graves. But the most well-preserved, and one of the very oldest Stone Age skeletons to be found in Norway, actually *was*, strangely enough, buried in a midden, a pile of rubbish or kitchen waste from that period—Stone Age compost, in other words.

The boy, who was buried just over 8,000 years ago in Vistehola, a cave near the city of Stavanger in southwest Norway, was about fifteen years old when he died. He was heavily built, but short for his age, even among his contemporaries. Being a coastal dweller, he ate lots of fish and larger marine mammals, but his diet had been varied and had also included fowl and game, wild plants, nuts, and roots, as well as shellfish and sea snails. We find remains of all these in the large middens the trappers left, both inside and outside the cave. The boy was buried among the remains of all the things he had eaten during his life.

The Viste Boy's grave is not unique. Being buried in kitchen waste seems to have been one of several possible ways you could depart this world in Stone Age Scandinavia. Usually, however, only small pieces of human remains dating from this time are ever unearthed: a small finger, a tooth, or a skull fragment. Bone pieces like these are also found in middens, or scattered around the settlement, seemingly at random. Archaeological investigations suggest that similar human bone fragments can be found in more than half of the Old Stone Age settlements located in Scandinavia. Fragmented human bones have also been found near the Viste Boy. These bones—which belonged to someone other than the buried boy—were not found as part of a grave. Nor were similar finds in a number of other caves and rock shelters dated from roughly the same time. A. W. Brøgger, the first archaeologist to excavate Vistehola in 1907, believed that such bone remains could be linked to cannibalism—if not specifically at Viste, then at least in the similar cases found in Denmark and Sweden. More recent interpretations have linked these fragmented remains to graves that are no longer recognizable as graves, and also to the use of human bones as "amulets," or even the possibility that bones and skulls were used as symbolic or religious objects in a kind of Stone Age "skull cult."

Who was chosen for burial in or outside the rubbish heap, or who fell victim to a skull cult (or was deprived of a grave in some other way), is difficult to hypothesize around when the circumstances occurred so long ago. And while there are so few of these graves, the questions that arise from our encounters with them often outnumber the answers we get. But as we move further forward in time, the more graves there are for us to study. We believe we know more about the lifestyle, beliefs, and era of the Vikings than we do about the first hunters to venture this far north. This is partly because of what we have learned from the hundreds of thousands of graves associated with Scandinavia's old Norse population. Calculations based on this material may, however, indicate that there are still too few of these graves—compared with other settlement finds and the assumed number of inhabitants on the farms—for them to be truly representative of the actual population. Some believe that we are "missing" perhaps as much as 50 percent of the graves one could expect to find given the circumstances. But what does that actually mean?

Considering the highly varied burial practices we see in Norway throughout the Iron Age, it is not hard to imagine that many people may have been buried in such a manner that it is now impossible to distinguish between them and untouched nature. We cannot tell if a body was burned if the ashes were scattered to the wind, or dumped in the sea; there is no archaeological material to read from. The same of course applies to a whole series of other more or less well-known death rituals, such as the Zoroastrians' Tower of Silence, where a corpse is eaten by birds of prey.

Another possibility, which to us perhaps seems even stranger, is that some people were given neither a grave nor any other form of ritual transition between life and death. We cannot give a clear answer as to who among the Viking population was buried, and who might not have been. We find both elaborate graves, containing tools, weapons, jewelry, textiles, and other grave goods, and quite basic cremation graves, without so much as a hairpin in them. Nothing about them suggests that high status, wealth, or gold was a criterion for burial after death. However, it is important to remember that society in the Nordic region during Viking times practiced slavery and a significant part of the population was unfree—with no rights over their bodies, their work, or their possessions. Could it be that they also had no right to a resting place after death? Is it this section of the population whose graves we cannot find?

The Arab long-distance traveler Ahmad Ibn Fadlan is today known as the author of one of the most important contemporary texts we have describing Vikings in the tenth century. Ibn Fadlan wrote about his experiences while traveling as a diplomatic envoy from the caliph in Baghdad to the Bulgarians who lived along the river Volga, in present-day Russia, in 921 and 922 CE. On his journey he encountered a trading people which he called the "Rus," and whom most experts now agree must have been an East European branch of Scandinavian Vikings. As an eyewitness account from this period, the text has become a fabulous source (Ibn Fadlan wrote about what he had personally seen and experienced, unlike many later scribes, who recounted old stories that they had heard from others). Among other things, he was fascinated by Viking funeral rituals, a theme we will return to in Chapter Nine. While kings, warriors, and chieftains would be honored with elaborate ceremonies after their deaths, Ibn Fadlan reported that slaves who fell ill and died on the journey were simply left along the way, like rubbish.

SO, AFTER A long detour covering thousands of years, we can safely say—as many previous generations will attest—that being *buried in garbage* is not the same as being *treated like garbage*, although there are long traditions of both throughout human history. But in a way, it was this distinction that Katrina Spade had to create public acceptance for when she started work on bringing her human-composting idea to life.

Precisely how she would be able to do that was less clear. Just like Capsula Mundi, Spade's project was initially both sympathetic and unrealistic, and it would still be a project on an academic drawing board today had she not been so determined to make her "Tower of Death" a reality. Many obstacles remained before that could happen, not least several changes to the laws and regulations around funerals. And before Spade could hope to do that, she had to convince bureaucrats and lawmakers that she knew what she was talking about—which, in 2013, she didn't.

To design a composting system that was guaranteed to work on humans, Spade began collaborating with forensic scientists and biologists. In her book *From Here to Eternity*, Caitlin Doughty describes a visit Spade made to an experimental research center in North Carolina, a so-called "body farm" where forensic scientists leave corpses outside, in a fenced-off landscape, to see how they decompose in various natural environments. Spade had been looking for the most effective "recipe" that would ensure the most comprehensive breakdown in the shortest possible time. When we spoke in 2018, Spade told us that the collaboration between scientists and burial innovators was absolutely crucial to the development of her project. At the same time, the meetings revealed a fairly significant cultural difference, as Doughty writes in her book. When Spade initially struggled to create fully composted matter, she was advised to chop the body up first, or add urine to the existing compost. These solutions are very practical because they speed up disintegration. But they were quite quickly rejected. Convincing people to deviate from established burial customs was hard enough as it was, without telling them that the corpse needed to be cut up and soaked in urine.

Spade's project was met with lots of interest, and lots of opposition. One critic was conspiracy-theory blogger Mike Adams, who feared that the urban, liberal, middle-class hunger for organic, home-grown vegetables would lead to "the forced euthanasia of the elderly so their corpses can be thrown on the compost heap," and that the project would be a way for the authorities to greenwash mass murder.

By collaborating with the scientists in North Carolina and elsewhere, Spade eventually managed to find a formula that produces

the fastest possible breakdown of corpses. Using the right combination of nitrogen, carbon, moisture, and microorganisms, the
temperature of the compost can be increased to 140°F (60°C), making
decomposition happen quickly and with barely any smell.

Gaining acceptance for the principle of human composting
became gradually easier—it is of course just a faster version of
what happens in the ground, and without a coffin. But the actual
building—the "death tower"—turned out to be a bigger problem.
Putting loved ones in a compost heap containing several other
bodies was considered unsafe and far, far too strange. When we
spoke, Spade told us that she was in the process of developing a
more individualized model. The result is somewhat like a beehive,
where each corpse is placed in its own cell. When the composting
is finished, after thirty days, the bereaved can be certain that the
soil they take home with them will have come from *their* loved one.

After this modification, the project—now named Recompose—
took off. With help from a number of backers, including the author
Margaret Atwood, Spade raised close to $700,000. In 2019, the pro-
ject was approved by the state legislature in Washington. And in the
winter of 2020—after a new funding round had managed to collect
an additional $6.75 million—the project was launched at a facility
outside Seattle. Spade had accomplished what Capsula Mundi had
been unable to: after thirty days, the bereaved are invited to collect
as much of the roughly 100 gallons of soil as they want, and take
it home where they can scatter it in the garden or use it to plant a
tree. Any soil not taken by the bereaved is otherwise used as a soil
improver in Bells Mountain, a 700-acre (285 ha) conservation area
outside Seattle where you can sit quietly, under a tree perhaps,
and listen to the birdsong, while contemplating death—and the
life that lives on.

7

UP IN SMOKE

As well as the soil-bound dead, modern cemeteries in Europe and North America also include cremation graves, which contain the deceased's ashes instead of a whole body. When you walk around the graveyard surrounding our house, nothing about the actual plots indicates whether they contain coffins or urns—in the cemetery all the stones are gray, with inscriptions telling you when the deceased was born and died, but not whether they were burned or buried. Still, it's quite easy—if you know a bit about cemetery logic at least—to identify the different sections. Coffin graves require—without always getting it—good soil conditions, and not least plenty of space. In the coffin sections, the standard space between the graves is over 10 feet (3 m), while a grave's width is at least 5 feet (1.5 m), and almost twice that if it's a double or family grave. Urn graves, however, take up far less space, since the urns can hold no more than a gallon of material. They can be interred in less favorable terrain, almost regardless of soil conditions and topography, provided you can dig or drill a 3-foot-deep (90 cm) hole about 8 inches (20 cm) in diameter. In Oslo North Cemetery there are urn graves in a number of places; on the southwest side of the chapel, where the gravestones are close together; in small, well-maintained mini-plots on the slope below our house; and on the small wooded mound southwest of our house, where the graves are more loosely arranged.

In recent years, cremation has become increasingly common in Norway, as it has in most Western industrialized—and fairly secular—countries. Nationwide, it is gradually catching up with coffin burials: in 2019 cremations accounted for 44 percent of all funerals. In 2020, the first year of the COVID-19 pandemic, there was a record-breaking 5 percent increase in cremations compared with the previous year. In the biggest cities and in the suburbs, it is already the dominant practice—more than 75 percent of all the dead in these places allow themselves to be burned.

Despite the recent upswing in most Western countries, cremation is by no means a new practice. Over the course of time, traditions related to inhumation graves (that is, when the corpse is buried in the ground, with or without a coffin) and ash or cremation graves have constantly alternated. In some places, cremation seems to have been dominant for long periods of time. At other times it seems to have been a rarity, something reserved for special individuals. There have also been long periods—such as now, in the present day—where the two practices have co-existed as two available options that users selected according to their status, or cultural or religious affiliation. Sometimes, we can assume, the decision would have been based on personal preference; we cannot be certain that our ancestors were necessarily more governed by religious or cultural practices than we are today.

The earliest known cremation graves can be dated back 40,000 years, to prehistoric times. In Europe, we know that our ancestors have burned their dead, at regular and irregular intervals, since the last part of the Stone Age. Around 1300 BCE, in the period just before the transition from the Older to the Younger Bronze Age, it became the dominant burial practice. From the five-hundred-year period we call the pre-Roman Iron Age—between 500 BCE and

1 CE—cremation graves are virtually the only ones found in the Norwegian archaeological material.

In early medieval written sources we find apparent justifications for the Iron Age cremations. In Snorri Sturluson's *Ynglinga saga*, we can read what is often referred to as "Odin's law":

> Odin established the same law in his land that had been in force in Asaland. Thus he established by law that all dead men should be burned, and their belongings laid with them upon the pile, and the ashes be cast into the sea or buried in the earth. Thus, said he, every one will come to Valhalla with the riches he had with him upon the pile; and he would also enjoy whatever he himself had buried in the earth.

In other words, cremation was a way of winding up one's estate: cleaning up after one's worldly existence and preparing for the transition to the next phase. But despite Odin's stern command, archaeological finds show that the reality was more complex: throughout the latter part of the Iron Age, we find both inhumation graves and cremation graves used interchangeably, often side by side.

However, since Christianity became the norm, around the twelfth century, people in Norway—as in most other Christian countries—were almost exclusively buried as corpses. While there are many cases of heathen traditions, holy places, stories, customs, and iconography being adopted by the new religion during the transition to Christianity, the Christian burial customs represented a definite break. The original concept of resurrection on Judgment Day demanded the corpse be complete in order for it to rise from the dead and go to heaven.

Although anyone taking a moment of reflection might have suspected that reassembling a corpse—after tens, hundreds, or even thousands of years—would be difficult, we still insisted on burying our dead, and continued to view cremation as both sinful and dishonorable. In burning the corpse, you also burned the possibility of salvation; being burned was an additional punishment, a double death sentence reserved for heretics, witches, and others who had clearly been allies with the forces of darkness and therefore deserved to have their path to salvation and resurrection blocked as well. The Catholic Church did not accept cremation until 1963, but even then it was with a disclaimer stating that "this choice must not have been made through 'a denial of Christian dogmas, the animosity of a secret society, or hatred of the Catholic religion and the Church.'"

While pre-Christian cremation and the Christian ban on cremation both might have been religiously motivated, the renewed interest in cremation in the late 1800s and early 1900s was part of a secular and provident belief in modernization. By adopting technical innovations and the logic of the industrial revolution, using modern and efficient incinerators, it was possible to ensure better public health, a lower risk from infectious diseases, and a far more rational use of the limited space in the cities. A new understanding of hygiene and innovations within the medical profession could help reduce the risk of arbitrary death and increase life expectancy. Cremation would help solve the problem of death. Preventing the dead from being a health hazard for the living had long been a challenge, and the problem had only increased in line with the rising levels of urbanization.

Cremation also offered the deceased another form of dignity, the dignity of being finished off by a purpose-built machine rather than slowly disintegrating into worm food.

Even after the change in law legalizing the practice, cremations were for many years difficult to carry out: the equipment to conduct the cremations was expensive, it was hard to get permission to build crematoriums close to cities, and in many places the procedure was allowed only in cases where the body had been subject to autopsy. The celebrated writer Camilla Collett had to be transported to Stockholm, Sweden, for her cremation. Before her death, Collett wrote about her desire to be cremated: "From my earliest years, the usual method of burial has filled me with Horror and Revulsion." Perhaps a young Camilla had found a rotting moose calf in the forest, too! Or was this horror and disgust triggered by the Victorians' fear of being buried alive? The desire to avoid premature burial was highlighted as one of several benefits among supporters of cremation when the new practice was legalized in many countries in the late 1800s.

In *The Work of the Dead* (2015), historian Thomas W. Laqueur tells the story of modern cremation. Here he discusses, among other things, one of the medical challenges of the Enlightenment: how do you establish that a person is well and truly dead and not just temporarily lifeless? Death as a diagnosis became particularly relevant from the 1740s after a small eight-page pamphlet was translated from Latin (*An mortis incertae signa*) into French, then English (*The Uncertainty of the Signs of Death*), and finally German in 1754—it was also expanded by several hundred pages between each of the different editions, and appended with the revealing subtitle *And the Evil of Premature Burial and Embalming*. What might be understood as one of several symptoms of a heightened awareness and belief in more scientific principles where body and soul are concerned led to an almost mythical level of public anxiety. This fear of suspended animation and premature burials was reinforced throughout the

1800s as popular culture and the mass media reveled in claustro-phobic descriptions and gruesome stories, about both the living dead and those buried alive. Gothic literature, which emerged in England at the end of the 1700s, continued to inspire writers and poets in Europe and the United States well into the 1800s. The most memorable were often about "scientific" monstrosities like Frankenstein's monster, created from old body parts and brought to life by a strange scientific spark, and bloodthirsty nocturnal monsters like Dracula, who routinely spent his days sleeping in a tomb. On the border between fantasy and reality, myth and science, was also the anxiety and depiction of being buried alive—Edgar Allan Poe's "The Premature Burial" (1844) is one such example.

The fear of being buried alive—according to several contemporary stories and eyewitness accounts—was very widespread and not entirely unwarranted. For example, in 1824, one John MacIntire is said to have recounted his own experience where, following a long illness, he entered a form of trance before being declared dead and subsequently buried. As luck would have it, he was dug up again shortly after by grave robbers. Later, as he lay on the dissection table in the anatomy room, his trance was broken—to the horror of the onlookers—when the lecturer plunged the scalpel into his gut. It is perhaps not an entirely credible story, but that did not prevent MacIntire's spectacular tale from being widely circulated in the press and other printed media.

In 1896, Edward Perry Vollum, a doctor who is also said to have been almost buried alive, published along with William Tebb and Walter Hadwen the self-help book *Premature Burial: How It May Be Prevented*, in which they claim to have documented over two hundred cases of people being buried alive in England alone in the decades before publication. In the same year that the book was published, Tebb and Hadwen founded the London Association for the Prevention of Premature Burial. The association's aim was to raise public awareness about what they considered a major social problem, but it also worked politically to gain approval for a legally required death certificate before a possible funeral.

Tebb and Hadwen's endeavors, to legislate that all deaths must be confirmed and formalized by a qualified doctor, perhaps stemmed from the diagnostic challenges that were defined in the 1700s, and which ordinary laypeople at least could not be expected to master. A weak pulse and faint breathing could be difficult things to identify and understand. The law was debated but never passed. However, public anxiety continued, and the prevailing trend at the time—which leant partly towards morbid romanticism and partly towards the science and modernity of the new age—facilitated a long series of inventions that would enable anyone who was mistakenly buried to communicate with the outside world or help them escape if they woke up. Varyingly ingenious patents for coffin alarms, ventilation systems and/or lids that could be opened from the inside were approved during the latter half of the 1800s and the early 1900s, and we have seen almost a continuation of this tradition among the approved patents—as recently as 2010 and 2015—for audiovisual systems that enable both the dead in the coffin and the bereaved to "listen" to the same music or sounds, and "see" the same images.

However, just how many people actually allowed themselves to be buried in these special coffins is less well known. When William Tebb himself died in 1917, he was careful to insure himself against his biggest fear using a different, and perhaps more effective method: he requested that his corpse be kept for a week, until there were visible signs of decay, before being cremated.

IN FRANCE, CREMATION was legalized as early as 1795, during the French Revolution. Back then the funeral pyre was seen as an alternative to the Christian dogma and "tyranny of the church" when it came to matters of death—it alluded to the exalted ideals of antiquity, and the ancient Romans who were known to have burned their dead, although in practice they had many different burial customs. However, when Napoleon came to power in 1801, he banned cremation, and it was not re-legalized in France until 1889, when the secularists had once more gained the upper hand. By this time, around the turn of the century, cremation technology had improved significantly and several other European nation-states had also legalized the practice.

The simplest form of cremation takes place on an open fire. As a rule, the body is placed in the middle of the bonfire surrounded by plenty of wood. When traditional cremations use a permanent location, the site will often be equipped with a grate or some other means of providing a strong flow of air. It ensures a high temperature, faster and cleaner combustion, and fewer remains at the end. This method is still practiced in several parts of India. In her book *From Here to Eternity: Traveling the World to Find the Good Death*, Caitlin Doughty writes about modern American cremation cooperatives, where members of the local community gather and cremate their dead on a similar outdoor funeral pyre.

When Lodovico Brunetti, a late nineteenth-century Italian professor of anatomical pathology, wanted to devise a cremation method so effective that only a minimal amount of ash and bones remained, he was fascinated and inspired by the relatively small cremation urns from antiquity. After a series of experiments conducted between 1869 and 1873, using both "traditional" pyres and an iron structure where dismembered parts of the body were placed in different levels, Brunetti concluded that it was not possible to achieve complete combustion of a body using fire alone. By looking to the metal industry, and the technology that would soon revolutionize steel production in the late 1860s, he developed an incinerator that would intensify the temperature by reverberating the heat back at the coffin and body from a vaulted ceiling. Combustion would then occur at an extremely high temperature indirectly— that is, without the body being touched by the flames or the fuel. Using this method, Brunetti managed to reduce the body of a 55-year-old man weighing 100 pounds, or 45 kg (the man had been very ill and emaciated when he died), to 4 pounds (1.8 kg) of ash in approximately two hours. Like modern entrepreneurs, he took his *appareils à réverbération* to a trade fair—the 1873 Vienna World's Fair to be precise—where he showed off his invention to an audience hungry to experience what progress the future could offer. Here he pointed and explained, and captured the interest of Sir Henry Thompson, the renowned urologist and personal surgeon to Kings Leopold I and II of Belgium.

Thompson was so impressed that he established the British Cremation Society in 1874, the first association of its kind to support the cause of cremation. He also continued to experiment and improve the technology behind the innovative cremation oven, sometimes collaborating with William Siemens, a renowned electrical engineer and brother of Werner von Siemens, who founded the well-known industrial company of the same name.

OSLO'S FIRST CREMATORIUM was established at Oslo West Cemetery in 1909. This was made possible thanks to a large financial donation from A. T. Gløersen, a wealthy forester who, on his death in 1904, bequeathed 50,000 kroner (roughly $5,000) for the building of a crematorium with its own columbarium, a hall for storing and displaying the urns. The circular building, built in the Art Nouveau style, is now used as Oslo West Cemetery's old chapel. Some of the older urns still remain in their niches. The artist Emanuel Vigeland decorated its walls and vaulted ceiling with beautiful frescoes, including a series of eight paintings in the dome that depict the life of a couple from the time they meet each other until they meet God after death. Emanuel, who was perhaps always in the shadow of his older brother, the renowned sculptor Gustav Vigeland, is otherwise best known for what he referred to as his life's work: a mausoleum in honor of himself. Today Tomba Emmanuelle, located in Oslo, is open to the public as a museum. Placed inside the impressive monument, just above the low entrance door, is Emanuel's urn. All who visit must bow their head to him on their way out.

AS WE HAVE SEEN, modern cremation is associated with the innovations and technological developments of industry during the last half of the 1800s. That cremation and metallurgical processes may have been connected also during prehistoric times is perhaps less well known, but it just as immediately makes sense when we consider the high temperatures required for burning an entire person to ashes. Osteoarchaeological investigations—archaeological studies of bones—could indicate that many of those who were burned for burials during the Nordic Bronze and Iron Ages were burned at higher temperatures than the standard used now. Today's cremation ovens maintain temperatures between 1,500 and 1,800°F (800 and 1,000°C). Investigations carried out on more than 1,000 cremation contexts, from the Bronze and Iron Ages in southern and eastern Norway, show that many of the bones have been burned at temperatures between 1,800 and 2,300°F (1,000 and 1,300°C). Such temperatures cannot usually be achieved using traditional outdoor funeral pyres. So how did they do it?

Archaeologist Terje Østigård has suggested that the art of cremation may have been closely related to crafts that required expertise and special knowledge about fire and heat—like the melting and casting of metal, for example. The melting points of the various metals and alloys that a Bronze or Iron Age blacksmith would have been able to control varies mostly within the same temperature range that will effectively burn a corpse, and reaching and maintaining such high temperatures for any length of time requires both knowledge and experience. It is unlikely that a random relative of the deceased would have been able to construct an equally effective funeral pyre without any kind of expert help. Was the prehistoric blacksmith perhaps also some kind of ritual specialist and fire master in charge of cremations? Perhaps the burning of the dead, in some cases, was even a part of the smelting and casting process? "The flesh as a fuel smelts together technology and cosmology," writes Østigård. Whatever the case may be, it is interesting that the introduction of a proper cremation burial custom in Scandinavia coincided with the transition from stone technology to an increasingly advanced form of metal technology.

Another archaeologist, Terje Gansum, who has collaborated with a blacksmith to produce iron and steel as it would or could have been made in the Viking Age, has also hypothesized about the possible convergence of the craftsman's technology and ritual cremation: when making steel out of iron for weapons and tools, the iron must go through a series of meticulously controlled processes, one of which involves adding carbon to the metal. The remains after a cremation are essentially pure carbon. So let us then imagine that the carbon added during the production of a sword came from the remains of an important family member, a respected warrior, or a feared and powerful animal, for that matter. Might it not give the weapon certain properties? A "personality" maybe, or willpower? We know that the Vikings gave their swords names: we have seen them etched as runes into the steel or hilts on some of the swords that have been found. There are also several named swords that play important roles in the various sagas that were handed down as oral narratives from the same period. And we find broken swords in the archaeological material—burned on the pyre, bent or broken, "killed" perhaps, or rendered harmless, before being placed in the grave along with their owner—or companion?

What we can be certain of, at least, is that something was done to the bones after the funeral pyre burned out. In cremation graves from this period, we find far less bone and ash than one would expect from a burned adult body. The usual amount of ash left by a fully grown man is around 10 pounds (4.5 kg); slightly less for a fully grown woman. In archaeological contexts we usually find only 10 to 20 percent of that amount. The same goes for those contexts where the bones were collected and buried in an urn or some other container. However, archaeological contexts can vary far beyond what we today associate with "a grave." Sometimes the bones are found neatly cleaned and sorted, or placed in a clay pot, or a bronze cauldron; sometimes it is just a fistful or a small bundle wrapped in a cloth or a leather bag. On other occasions we find bones and ashes thrown together, with seemingly no thought given to what went in and what did not. Sometimes we find jewelry and other items in the containers, but not always. The items themselves can show signs of having been close to the fire, but it is just as likely that they were placed among the bones after—as complete and undamaged as they were in life. The containers could be buried in the ashes after the cremation, or at an entirely different location— often (like the child we remember from Egtved Girl's grave) far from the actual cremation site. Sometimes we find urns deposited in the burial mounds of people who had been buried many generations earlier. On other occasions we find no containers whatsoever, just bones and ashes, cleaned and uncleaned, with and without other items. But cremated human bones are also found in totally different contexts—in the post holes of house foundations, in hearths, in rubbish heaps, sometimes apparently scattered on farmland or in smelting furnaces.

Scattering ashes to the wind, into running water, or upon the open sea are familiar practices today and may well have been practiced at other times too. The one thing we know for sure is that there was not one single practice of cremating the dead during this period of history. On the contrary, the funeral pyre made it possible for the bereaved to take the remains of their dead to an infinite number of different places and situations that mattered to them. Perhaps that is why we never find all the ashes that we would expect. Was it perhaps important to place the bones and ashes in different places in the landscape, or in places that meant different things to the deceased or the surviving family? Were these decisions predetermined by different rules and norms, or were they more pragmatic, random, or even totally unique to each of the deceased, and to each of the bereaved?

It is also possible to imagine that although the person's life had ended, it still determined how the body would be treated in death. Age, status, social and economic function, or even the cause of death can place different demands on what is perceived to be an "appropriate" funeral. For example, Østigård refers to how, among

Nepal's Hindus, cremation is reserved for certain groups in different stages of the life cycle. Boys who have undergone the rites of passage from childhood to manhood are cremated; younger boys are buried. Women will be cremated if they are married; unmarried women will not.

The main principle among the Abrahamic religions—Judaism, Christianity, and Islam—is for the corpse to be buried. Hinduism and Buddhism practice cremation as a rule, with some local variations which include cave and forest burials among some Chinese groups and the much talked-about, but not widely practiced, tradition of "sky burial" in Tibet, where the corpses are chopped up and left outside to be eaten by vultures.

In the Hindu tradition, cremation is something that is done out in the open, ideally on a funeral pyre beside a river. The head of the deceased will normally be shaved, and they will be washed and dressed—usually in white, or red for a woman if her husband is still alive—with the thumbs and big toes tied together. The corpse will then be placed with the legs pointing south on a platform or a stone slab, along with plenty of dry wood. After being sprinkled with ghee—clarified butter—the fire will be lit. Ancient custom considers it desirable for the deceased's head to explode, allowing onlookers to see the person's soul being set free. If the fire is hot enough this can create a striking visual effect, since the brain contains around 60 percent fat and easily ignites. If the head fails to explode by itself, it is normally the eldest son's task to crush the skull. After the cremation, the ashes are usually thrown into the river.

In the Hindu tradition, death and its rituals are not hidden away but a public event visible for all to see. The city of Varanasi on the Ganges—considered the holiest city on the sacred river—is a place where people go to die, hoping that in making this journey they will achieve *moksha*, liberation from the eternal cycle of rebirth. Funeral pyres constantly line the riverbank, where the dead are visible before and during the various cremations, and crowds of tourists, pilgrims, hawkers, and wood carriers move freely between them. It is hard to imagine anything further removed from the modern Western cremation as it has been practiced for the last century, where the point seems to be applying the maximum amount of heat to achieve the most efficient cremation, albeit surrounded by a seemingly cold and impersonal ceremony.

For over fifty years, Oslo had just one crematorium in the west of the city. Then, in 1961, the East Crematorium opened. In both cases, the cremation ovens themselves were located in the cellar, hidden from the eyes of the mourners. When the ceremony in the chapel ended, the priest, or whoever officiated, could press a button and the coffin would descend below floor level. Once the mourners had left the chapel, the coffin was lowered further into the cellar. You would see no more of the deceased until the urn containing their ashes arrived a few days later. In many cases, the funeral reception was held somewhere else, and the body incinerated in the crematorium's cellar without the bereaved participating in any part of the process.

This changed in 2009, when a new state-of-the-art crematorium opened at Alfaset, a few miles east of our house and the neighboring cemetery. The most important reason for building this new crematorium was the same one that led to the plastic-bag-burial debacle: concerns about pollution from the cremation ovens. Smoke from the chimneys had always been one of the criticisms regarding cremation, and not just during the period when the coffins were being lined with tar paper. In the period that followed, there were numerous complaints from local residents, and increasingly strict rules against air pollution made it clear that the old ovens would have to be replaced. A former employee of the department for burials described to us how thick, foul-smelling black smoke often billowed from the chimneys when a new coffin was placed in the oven. "In autumn and winter, when the air outside was cold and damp, the smoke would settle, and you could smell it on the ground. It could be quite overwhelming and unpleasant if there were mourners waiting right outside." The old crematoria were also impractical to operate; they were spread across multiple levels, connected by narrow corridors, and inappropriately laid out.

The incinerators at the new crematorium are computer-operated and as precisely calibrated as industrial melting furnaces, and the requirements for purifying the emissions are so strict that the smoke is said to be cleaner than the air outside, which is full of exhaust fumes from the nearby motorway. Before the new crematorium was built, it was agreed that much of it would be different from the existing facilities. The most important change was for the crematorium to be built on one floor, so that the coffins could be wheeled around without employees having to negotiate arduous and impractical level changes. The rooms they work in are light and airy. To a visitor, the most striking thing is how open the whole crematorium is. Instead of being hidden down in a cellar, the committal room faces the cemetery and is visible through clear glass walls. This allows daylight in—and makes it possible for anyone to witness the activity inside.

The best way to follow all of the proceedings is from the viewing room, which has a large window providing a clear view into not just the committal room but the cremation chamber itself. Members of Norway's small Hindu population had for years wanted to be able to perform cremations that were more in line with Hindu tradition. From the viewing room, you can watch the coffin being moved into the cremation chamber. Once inside, and by the time the chamber doors close, the coffin will have caught fire.

The viewing room was built particularly with the Hindu community in mind, but they are certainly not the only people who use it. Now that the option is available, it seems that there are many people who want to witness the actual cremation. The viewing room will normally be full of close family, while those unable to get inside are allowed to stand outside, along the glass wall, and look in from there.

As we were being shown around the crematorium, there were several cremations taking place. Seeing a coffin being moved into the chamber, watching it catch fire knowing that there is a body in there, and then, one hour later, observing the oven being emptied from the other side where another glass wall offers complete transparency, is a unique experience. Despite the high temperature used, what comes out is more than just ash. Bones—especially larger ones such as femurs, radial bones, and parts of the skull—will often come out too, still recognizable as once belonging to a human. These are collected and crushed in a separate bone-crushing machine with the horror-film name "the cremulator." Any remnants of jewelry, prosthetics, or similar effects are sent for recycling.

FIRE HAS BEEN with us for a long time, and while the crematoria have become increasingly modern and more technologically advanced, the principle has not changed: the corpse is exposed to a high temperature until nothing remains except the most vital component for the human body and most other living things—carbon—which looks almost no different to the charred remains of an animal or plant.

But this is no longer the only way to cremate. When mad cow disease—prion-based bovine spongiform encephalopathy—began ravaging Europe in the 1980s, hundreds of thousands of animals were euthanized to stop potentially diseased animals from entering the human food chain, where it can cause Creutzfeldt-Jakob disease, which leads to a slow and painful death. The disease is caused by a prion, which in simple terms is a malformed protein that multiplies and can have an incubation period of several years. The euthanized animals, however, remained a threat to public health even after their death. There was no safe way to dispose of the animal corpses: the cremation ovens were too small to handle a large cow or bull, let alone thousands of them. Most of the animals were burned, many of them in huge medieval-looking bonfires. One can safely say that this was a far from ideal practice: the bonfires used railway sleepers and other materials containing environmental toxins, and in many cases the animals exploded. The smell and air pollution led to a number of complaints from neighbors, but the biggest concern was the further spread of infection. Prions will not be eliminated unless the temperature of the fire is extremely high, so how could anyone be sure that it would not contaminate the groundwater, or be transmitted by airborne particles? Everyone who has raked through a burned-out campfire will know you always find something that was not properly incinerated. A prominent British environmental organization suggested using napalm, because it is clean-burning and reaches high temperatures without any undue emission of smoke.

As a result of the crisis, two American scientists developed a chemical method for dissolving carcasses using alkaline hydrolysis. In short, this involves placing the dead animal in a strongly alkaline liquid which is then heated. After a few hours the carcass has dissolved. The technique was not used to any great extent while mad cow disease was raging, but in the 2000s it was introduced as an alternative to human cremation, a process that is often referred to as "water cremation." In Scotland, biochemist Sandy Sullivan, who previously worked for a company that offered solutions for the disposal of cow carcasses and radioactive rabbits, has established the company Resomation, which has found ways of standardizing and commercializing the process. A number of similar companies have been established in the USA and Australia, too, and the method is now permitted in several countries.

When a human body has been water-cremated, it will have been broken down into its basic elements. All bacteria, viruses, prions—even DNA—will be gone. Like normal cremations, some of the large bones will occasionally be left, white and fragile, and they disintegrate when touched. The remaining ash is also white. And the leftover fluid can then be adjusted for pH and released into the sewer without causing any pollution.

WHILE THE RULES about what can be done with a corpse—for natural as well as cultural reasons—are very strict, there are fewer restrictions on what can be done with the ashes. Normally the urn containing the ashes will be buried in a cemetery and topped with a headstone, making it look confusingly similar to a coffin grave. In family graves, urns can be buried in plots that are intended for coffins, but obviously not the other way around, and in many places, depending on national and local regulations, it is permitted to scatter ashes at sea, or in rivers and waterways, or a countryside location, most often with the condition that the scattering is done in a sufficiently deserted area and does not resemble a "private grave." Regulators are keen to avoid a situation where the previous inhabitants of a building claim the right to return to the garden to be with Grandpa.

Cremation ashes can also be used as a memento. There are several websites selling urn jewelry, one of them being the "Together Forever" urn necklace, which includes a small container that allows you to carry around a few cubic centimeters of ashes. It has already sold out several times. "So hurry," says the product information, "before it's too late!"

8

PIECEMEAL AND DIVIDED

W hen the Catholic Church was allowed to re-establish itself in Norway in the 1840s following the original 1814 Constitution's ban on Catholic congregations, it soon became obvious that something was missing. Slowly, the small and relatively poor Catholic congregation grew, and a few years later—with the support of several donors, including the Italian-born Queen Josefine of Sweden and Norway—St. Olav's Cathedral was built at Hammersborg. This area, now in the city center, was back then on the outskirts of town, close to Our Saviour's Cemetery, about a mile south of where Oslo North Cemetery would be built a few decades later. The church was considered by many to be the most beautiful in the city.

Every year, on July 29—or for practical reasons often the following Sunday—St. Olav's Day is celebrated in memory of King Olav II Haraldsson, who is often credited with the Christianization of Norway. In 1861, Queen Josefine was present in the church, along with her former court chaplain, Laurentius J. Studach, who was now vicar apostolic and Catholic superior of the congregation. But what was missing that day was Olav himself.

The warrior king had been canonized only a year after being killed at the Battle of Stiklestad in 1030, and rumors that his corpse had magical powers began spreading soon after. Olav's adversary and killer, Tore Hund, is said to have been the first to claim that

Olav was holy—his own wounds had healed when blood from Olav's corpse ran onto his injured hand. There were also reports that Olav's hair and nails continued to grow after his death. His beard and hair were cut as good-luck talismans on several occasions postmortem, the last time being before Harald Hardrada traveled to Stamford Bridge in 1066. Useless in hindsight, you could say; the spectacular loss is considered the end of the Viking era.

In a 1955 edition of the Catholic magazine *St. Olav*, Johannes J. Duin cites what are supposed to be eyewitness accounts from the 1500s, all of which stress how Olav's face and body continued to be mysteriously unaffected by time; his flesh, skin, toes, and sinews unspoiled; and his teeth still in place. "A sweet air surrounded him, nothing repellent about it." Snorri Sturluson's account of the first opening of the coffin, a year after the day of death, seems eerily similar: "It gave off a wonderful scent." In the early Middle Ages, the king's remains were laid to rest behind the altar of Trondheim's main church, which later expanded and became Nidaros Cathedral. During the years of war and unrest, however, Olav's body is said to have been robbed by the Swedes, but later triumphantly returned to Trondheim. After the Reformation—when it became clear that people still worshipped the saint "in the Catholic manner"—his remains were finally buried. The exact location is unknown.

A constant theme among the descriptions of Olav's corpse—in addition to the nice smell—is that it had remained intact throughout all of the upheaval. At the same time, a reliquary containing what was claimed to be a bone from Olav's arm, Brachium Sancti Olaui, was sent south at some point during the Danish period of rule. When Josefine visited Norway in 1861, the piece was still at Denmark's National Museum in Copenhagen. Studach used the queen's visit to make a request: could the queen ask the Danish king to return the relic to Norway, where it undoubtedly belonged? It would presumably draw more attention to St. Olav, and perhaps even attract people to the small Catholic congregation. Josefine remained Catholic her entire life, despite the fact that Protestantism was the state religion in Sweden and Norway, and she used her royal connections to ask King Frederik vii for the relic, as a personal favor.

The following year, the relic was sent to Norway. The reliquary itself has a crystal embedded in the side of the container that allows viewers to see the bone within. What was believed to be Olav's arm was enclosed in a holster shaped like an upright hand.

There are quite a few things about the Olav relic that do not add up. The arm inside the case is in fact a leg bone, not an arm. Investigations also testify that the bone has never been buried, while Olav, according to the saga, was buried for a year before the coffin, with the fragrant corpse inside, exhumed itself from the ground. More recently, the bone has been the subject of a number of investigations. Whether it originally belonged to Olav is impossible to confirm, but scientific analyses have not found anything that suggests the opposite either: the bone does originate from a man aged between 25 and 35 who died sometime between 980 and 1040, and it also has signs of an arrow injury suffered during a battle that must have taken place several years before the person died. So it might indeed originate from a warrior.

It is not unusual for great men and women to be revered after their death. Their power and influence often grow in the following years, and they can become rallying points. Ever since the Holy Arm reliquary containing what could be Olav's shin bone arrived back in Norway it has been St Olav's Cathedral's most treasured object. But it certainly is not the only bone to have liberated itself from Olav's "complete and intact" body. In the 1300s, another was placed in a reliquary and sent to Björksta church in Sweden, and in the 1400s Trondenes church had a small copper box that likewise contained one of the saint-king's bones. There are also historical sources referring to the widespread trading of relics that went on before the Reformation, including a letter from the Bishop of Turku in Finland who, in the late 1400s, expressed his wish to acquire a piece of the saint-king's body for his church, in exchange for a piece of Finland's own patron saint, Henry. In more recent times, parts of Olav have also traveled as relics: in 2014, to celebrate the 1,000th anniversary of Olav's baptism at Rouen Cathedral, a piece of the shin bone was sent from the cathedral in Oslo to Rouen, where it is now one of the attractions, along with what is supposed to be the heart of Richard I.

If everyone wants a piece of you, the Christian goal for the body to remain complete and intact can be hard to reconcile with the wishes of the bereaved, whether they are fellow believers, followers, fans, or family. It can also present practical issues.

When the British explorer David Livingstone died while on an expedition in 1873 at Chipundu in present-day Zambia, it was immediately decided that his body should be returned to England. Livingstone was a national treasure, considered not just a great imperialist and humanist, but in many ways the epitome of the British Empire then spreading its version of civilization across ever larger parts of the globe. When he disappeared for several years in the 1860s, extensive rescue operations were launched to find him, one of which resulted in Henry Morton Stanley's famous greeting upon finding him in 1871: "Dr. Livingstone, I presume." Two years later, when he died, Livingstone's fellow travelers were sure that he deserved a grand funeral with full honors back home in London. But how would the body get there?

Chipundu has a tropical climate, and Livingstone died near the end of the rainy season. It was hot and humid, and the landscape was impossible to traverse. Reaching the coast meant a more than sixty-day journey through rugged terrain. They were, in other words, among the most unfavorable circumstances one could have for preserving a corpse. Had nature been allowed to take its course, his body would have disintegrated as quickly as the dead moose calf we found in southern Norway. At the time, chemical embalming of corpses was being practiced in the United States, but Livingstone's entourage in Chipundu lacked all of the necessary equipment and expertise. The solution to the problem was twofold: in order to transport the corpse home without it rotting, the heart and other internal organs were removed and buried at the current location, beneath a mupundu tree. The rest of Livingstone's body was cured and dried in the traditional way and transported, as a mummy, 1,000 miles (1,600 km) to the coast and then returned to London by boat. The final funeral took place at London's Westminster Abbey in April 1874, eleven months after Livingstone's death. No one knows if the body has yet turned to dust.

It was fitting for this great man's heart to be buried in Africa, a place he loved so much, while his body was returned to his homeland. Today, it still seems like an excessive amount of resources to be used on moving a corpse—several nameless members of the entourage died on the grueling and perilous journey transporting the body to the coast. But the tradition of having separate burials for the heart and the rest of the body goes back centuries. During the Crusades in the 1100s, a relatively rare, yet established, practice took shape in similar circumstances—a solution for especially prominent knights slain during a campaign. The knight's footmen could only be sure of getting paid for their mission (that is, following a nobleman to the Holy Land and back) if there was a body to show. So the knight's heart would be buried near where the crusader had fallen, and if that happened to be in or near Jerusalem, even better. The body was then usually stripped of flesh so that the skeleton could be transported home without having to deal with a ghastly pile of rotting soft tissue. But if the knight had any distinguishing features, it was important to preserve these for identification.

The Crusaders' solution to a practical—and potentially financial—problem gradually became a kind of fashion among the upper class. After hearing about the unfortunate saints whose hearts were buried in the Promised Land, others wanted to do likewise and arranged to have their own hearts sent to Jerusalem for burial. Eventually these heart burials were condemned by Pope Boniface VIII in 1299. However, although he threatened to excommunicate those who chose such burials, the practice continued.

Some wealthy noblemen even paid to have their bodies cut into several pieces that were then sent to different monasteries where monks would pray for a swift transit through purgatory and up to heaven—the idea being that the more monasteries you were at, the more prayers you would get. And since this was a service that the monasteries were generously paid for, the abbots not only accepted but actively encouraged it. For many believers it proved impossible to choose between the goal of respecting the sanctity of the body and its resurrection, and the idea that body parts associated with especially pious or even holy people had magical powers and could relieve suffering, heal, and perform miracles.

There were many who had a romantic approach to the distribution of body parts: the heart would be transported somewhere that had special meaning for the deceased, while the body would be buried where the person had worked. This treatment was also applied to one of Henry VIII's unfortunate wives, Anne Boleyn, who, after her execution, had made sure that her heart was sent to Erwarton in Suffolk, a place she had loved as a child; and the composer Frédéric Chopin, whose body was buried in the famous Père Lachaise cemetery in Paris, while his sister took his heart—reportedly preserved in brandy—back to the Church of the Holy Cross in Warsaw. Chopin is said to have suffered from his contemporaries' fear of being buried alive, and his last words on his deathbed were supposedly linked to this: "The earth is suffocating . . . As this cough will choke me, I implore you to have my body opened, so that I may not be buried alive." Maybe the distributing of his earthly remains was also meant to be a final insurance against coming back to life, helpless beneath the cold turf?

Dismemberment of the body was often done for practical, sentimental, and religious reasons, but it could also be politically motivated. As described vividly in Christopher Buckley's novel *The Relic Master* (2015), relics were often produced and sold to buyers who used them to boost their reputations. Some saints have so many bones spread around different locations that it shrouds their saintly deeds, not to mention their anatomy, in mystery. In Sicily the much-venerated bones of St. Rosalia, who saved Palermo from a plague five centuries after her death, have been found to come not from a human but a goat. In *Heavenly Bodies: Cult Treasures and Spectacular Saints from the Catacombs* (2013), Paul Koudounaris tells a story of a church who had a relic purported to be the brain of St. Peter; it turned out to be a calcified potato.

Several burial mounds in the Norwegian countryside have been named after the sagas' first king of Norway, Halfdan the Black. Snorri writes:

When his death was known and his body was floated to
Ringerike to bury it there, the people of most consequence
from Raumarike, Vestfold, and Hedemark came to meet it.
All desired to take the body with them to bury it in their
own district, and they thought that those who got it would
have good crops to expect. At last it was agreed to divide
the body into four parts. The head was laid in a mound at
Stein in Ringerike, and each of the others took his part
home and laid it in a mound; and these have since been
called Halfdan's Mounds.

Snorri no doubt knew about several of these Halfdan mounds
during his time, but it is unclear if that is because Halfdan actually *is* buried in several places or because many people understood
the benefit of having Norway's first king buried in their community. Archaeological investigations of one of the mounds indicate
that it pre-dates Halfdan the Black's fall through the ice by several
hundred years.

In Mexico, the much hated and ridiculed politician and general Antonio López de Santa Anna, who was president for eleven
separate terms—during which time the country lost half its terri-
tory—is best known for a spectacular piece of political theatre:
during the so-called "pastry war" against the French—*la guerra de los
pasteles*—López de Santa Anna lost a leg in battle, and this leg was
then buried during a grand state funeral, which is said to have been
a decisive factor in his making yet another comeback as president.

Dismemberment as a policy can equally be used as a demonstration of power towards one's enemies and by aggressors in war.
The leg was later exhumed and dragged through the streets by his
political opponents.

In 1592, Japan invaded Korea as part of a broader plan to conquer first China, and then East Asia as a whole. The war in Korea—the Imjin War—lasted six years and is estimated to have caused the deaths of up to a million Koreans, perhaps as much as one-third of the population. The Japanese samurai warriors sent home large quantities of war booty such as porcelain, precious metals, and jewelry. It was also common at the time to send the severed head of an opponent home, like a cross between a trophy and proof of a mission accomplished. But in this war the custom proved too impractical due to both the large number of casualties and the long distances involved. Victors would instead cut off their victims' noses, and in some cases their ears as well. The noses and ears were then pickled in barrels, as one did with meat and fish, and sent home. At one point these trophies became such coveted status symbols that some samurai would cut off the noses and ears of living civilians, and in the post-war years it is said to have been common to see rural Koreans with their noses cut off.

Tens of thousands of noses and ears are today buried in a 10-meter-high burial mound associated with the temple Hōkō-ji in Kyoto, where the followers of the Japanese warlord Toyotomi Hideyoshi still commemorate his victories. "One cannot say that cutting off noses was so atrocious by the standard of the time," one plaque stated, before it was removed due to protests from Japan's Korean minority, who held a different opinion. Another, previously forgotten burial mound estimated to contain the noses of around 20,000 Koreans was discovered outside Osaka in 1983. Nine years later, the noses were returned to Korea, where they were cremated and buried.

It is easy to appreciate why the noses have become so important: they are all that remains of people who have otherwise been wiped out. A more distinctive tradition that arose—and probably disappeared as well—in the USA at the end of the 1800s was the creation of special "accident cemeteries," which were often linked to the construction of the railways. One such cemetery was in Denison, Texas. "It is used for the burial of hands, legs, fingers, and other body parts of persons crushed and mutilated by the railway cars in a manner requiring amputation," wrote the *Dallas Morning Post* in an 1891 article reproduced in *The Victorian Book of the Dead*. On one side of the square there was a kind of field hospital where these amputations were carried out, while the other part of the square was used to bury the severed body parts. "Two weeks ago little Johnny Wells' legs were placed in the ground in this unique graveyard, and this morning E. R. McCain's foot was lain to rest in the same place."

More recently, our friend the author Åsne Seierstad told us about an Iraqi soldier she met at the start of the Iraq War in 2003 who had buried his amputated leg in the cemetery, beside the graves of his relatives, where it will lie until he too is eventually buried there. Certain Muslim minorities in the Balkans and in Turkey have a similar tradition where, after *khitan*—circumcision—the foreskin will be buried in the local cemetery.

Can the soul find peace if the corpse is incomplete? The belief that it cannot was the rationale behind the additional sentence handed down to the mass murderer William Burke, who killed people in order to sell their bodies for use in Edinburgh's anatomy rooms in the early 1800s. Burke was hanged for his crimes, and his additional sentence was public dissection. His skin was used to bind a notebook, now part of the collections of the Royal College of Surgeons of Edinburgh and currently on display beside Burke's death mask in the Museum of Edinburgh. Anthropodermic bibliopegy—as the tradition of binding books with human skin is called—was a hobby for some nineteenth-century surgeons, and although it was not exactly a normal pastime, there are several examples of criminals ending up on their doctors' bookshelves, and in some cases their victims' bookshelves too. These examples of dismemberment after death are seen as unusual or totally unnatural to many within both Judeo-Christian and secular communities, although different parts of the practice have appeared numerous times throughout history. We have clung on to the notion that the body is inviolable, even as a corpse.

Many of us will shudder when we hear about hearts and bodies getting buried in different places, or even worse, disembodied noses and books bound in human skin. This notion is so deeply rooted that many people hesitate to register as organ donors. In some cultures, however, not only is body dismemberment accepted, it is an essential mortuary practice. In his influential and, in later years, controversial book from 1929, *The Sexual Life of Savages in North-Western Melanesia*, the anthropologist Bronisław Malinowski writes about the customs of a group of people he visited early in the 1900s, in the Trobriand Islands off the coast of Papua New Guinea. The Trobrianders are renowned in the field of anthropology, largely because of their belief that men play no role in the fertilization of women, and therefore have no blood ties with their children. Instead, the men contribute by ensuring that the child is formed properly, something the father and the father's family achieve by massaging the baby to shape its appearance. If you have ever wondered why children often resemble their father and their father's family, this could explain why. In short, the mother gives the child content, while the father gives it form. This distinction between content and form is also maintained after death, when the family on the mother's side will have to stay away from the corpse at all costs, while the family on the father's side—who are not considered blood relatives—are tasked with handling the remains. These tasks consist of elaborate ceremonies where the body is first buried, and then exhumed. The now rotting corpse will be inspected for signs of witchcraft before being cut into pieces. After that the bones will be cleaned, a process that involves, among other things, the sons sucking the marrow from them, explains Malinowski. "I have sucked the radius bone of my father; I had to go away and vomit; I came back and went on," he quotes one of the sons who was assigned to what he refers to as "a heavy, repugnant and disgusting duty." Nowadays we would also consider this an extremely dangerous duty, but what concerned the Trobrianders that Malinowski lived with more than anything was the risk of someone on the mother's side coming into contact with the deceased. The bones were then distributed among various family members and in-laws on the father's side and used as both decoration and even everyday objects. "I have seen the jawbone of a man with whom I had spoken a few days before dangling from the neck of his widow," writes Malinowski. Distant relatives and friends would get nails, locks of hair, and teeth. It was not only a way of stripping and dismantling the body; it de-created the body, stripping it of both content and form until it was finally transformed into something else—no longer a corpse or a close relative, but a memory, a piece of jewelry, an implement.

Because, after all, that is often what it's all about when we humans say farewell to our dead. All the applied practices are also inextricably linked to our beliefs about how life can and must continue for those who are left behind. The mortuary practice is a rite of passage—something that separates the dead from the living. The dead body is somewhere in between: it has a physical presence, but it is not part of the living world, nor is it yet in the otherworldly or abstract form, where we can mourn the dead, remember them, address them as ancestors, or forget them. Many of our beliefs about what awaits us after death—and how we might get there without placing our own or someone else's (after)life and peace of mind at risk—require the practical treatment of the body to be carried out in very specific ways.

WE HAVE BEEN traveling to Zanzibar with the family for many years. One of the first things you notice when you arrive in Stone Town is the abundance of crows that constantly steal food if given the chance. The crows are not native to the island, and one explanation for why someone deliberately brought them there—as they are not normally considered useful animals—is that they once served a purpose for the funeral rituals of what was then a not-insignificant minority of Zoroastrian Parsis.

Zoroastrianism is an ancient religion, possibly dating back more than 3,000 years. It was the leading religion in Persia until the Muslim conquest of the region in the mid-1500s; after that, the majority of Zoroastrians lived in India, in and around the area that is now the city of Mumbai. The group is often simply referred to as Parsis (from "Persians").

Central to Zoroastrian theology is a notion of purity—not least the importance of preserving the basic elements of water, earth, fire, and air to ensure that they are not contaminated. When someone dies, their body is considered extremely impure—contagious, almost—so it is important for the family to get rid of the body as quickly as possible. But it is also important that the corpse does not contaminate any of the four elements, which is obviously impossible if you choose any of the usual methods to dispose of the deceased. Burial is forbidden because it will pollute the soil; cremation is forbidden because it will contaminate the fire; and water and air have to be kept clean too. At the same time, trapped in its earthly body, is the soul, which longs to be set free so that it can go to heaven.

The solution to this was for the dead to be placed on the rocky slope of a mountain, where they would be devoured by birds of prey. However, the barren mountainsides were eventually abandoned in favor of a purpose-built burial tower, called the Tower of Silence. Corpses were then placed in the tower, where they would disappear as the birds fed on them. In most places these birds were vultures, which can strip a corpse of flesh in fifteen minutes and have long been referred to as nature's garbage collectors. The remaining bones would be left in the sun for a few extra days until they were bleached, and any trace of flesh was gone, before being gathered up and thrown into a pit in the middle of the tower. By this point, the soul was regarded as having moved on, and the remains were therefore pure and no longer posed any danger to the humans or the elements. The bones could be mixed with ash and then with soil.

There are almost no limits to the kind of mortuary practices that have arisen in different cultures, but what many of the most unusual of these have in common is that they are often practiced by people who live in relative isolation, such as the Trobriand people. But the Zoroastrians, who survived waves of persecution and Islamic missionary work, are essentially traders and live predominantly in large cities. Religious historian Kari Vogt, who lived in Mumbai in the 1970s, where there is a significant, albeit small, Zoroastrian minority that remembers how the Zoroastrian funerals would sometimes cause disputes with neighbors. "There were readers' letters in the newspaper every now and then," she said. "I remember one from a lady who wrote that she had been standing on the balcony hanging up clothes when a finger landed on her. The lady was shaken and thought it was time the Parsis found a more practical way of handling their dead."

When Parsis settled in Zanzibar, they quickly ran into trouble when disposing of the deceased. This island off the coast of East Africa no longer had any carrion birds that could do the work of eating the corpses. In other words, the Zoroastrians' customs were totally impractical for the location. Importing vultures was not considered an option. So an attempt was made to import crows, which did not have the same stigma as the larger carrion birds. Unfortunately, they were not as good at their job either. Vultures are specialist carnivores, while crows are opportunists that would sooner plunder a dustbin for a half-eaten kebab than wait for the next corpse to be delivered. After the Zanzibar Revolution in 1964, many of the Parsis fled the island—including Farrokh Bulsara, later known as Freddy Mercury—and today there are only a few families left. It has been a long time since traditional Zoroastrian funerals were performed in Zanzibar. When we visited the ancient Zoroastrian cemetery outside Stone Town, the Tower of Silence was closed. An elderly caretaker, who was using the building at the foot of the tower as a carpentry workshop, told us that over the last few decades a new custom had evolved as a kind of compromise: the corpses are placed in sealed boxes made out of cement or steel, which protect the elements from contamination while the hungry crows look elsewhere for food.

You can sense how traditions arise for practical reasons as well as religious ones, or how religious meaning and applied practice often go hand in hand, when visiting the Parsis' holy city of Yazd in modern-day Iran. The Zoroastrian cemetery in Yazd is a barren patch of rocky desert, entirely devoid of trees that could be used for cremation and with barely penetrable soil. The same goes for the mountains of Tibet, where a similar type of burial is still practiced. In the Tibetan sky burial, the body is taken to a sacred place in the mountains, where a *rogyapa* (meaning "body-breaker")—a sort of cross between a priest and a sanitation worker—chops the body up and feeds it to waiting vultures. When the vultures have finished eating, all that is left is bones, which are then crushed into powder, mixed with yak butter, and given to the vultures as a "second course." The whole ceremony usually takes less than one hour, and when it's over, there is nothing left.

In Mumbai, home to an estimated half of the world's 120,000 remaining practicing Parsis, a combination of hunting and pollution has wiped out the entire local population of vultures. Not least, it turns out that diclofenac, a medicine used to reduce inflammation in both humans and cows, has major consequences when it accumulates higher up the food chain. When vultures eat the carcasses of animals that have been given the drug, they die of kidney failure. The substance is considered one of the main reasons why India's vulture population has been almost totally wiped out since the early 1990s. Diclofenac was banned as a veterinary medicine in 2006, but is still permitted for humans, and in India's fairly unregulated pharmaceutical market, it is available in very large packs that are obviously meant for quadrupeds.

The lack of vultures has become a major problem for Mumbai's tiny Parsi community—which all started with a recent scandal. Since 1673, the Parsis' holy temple and *dhakma*—the Tower of Silence—has been located in the 1,000-acre (400 ha) Doongerwadi forest, which was also home to a large colony of vultures. When the vultures died out, the funerals carried on as usual. Apart from an uptick in neighbors' complaints about the smell coming from the facility, few within the congregation had any idea of what the conditions inside the *dhakma* were like. But in 2006 a member of the congregation, Dhun Baria, published photos that she had taken after sneaking into the tower. Baria had heard rumors that the conditions within the walls were disgraceful. Someone had told her it would take as long as a year for her recently deceased mother to decompose. She therefore entered the grounds—which normally only a small group of professional undertakers were permitted to access—to find out what had happened to her mother's body. The pictures she took showed tens, perhaps hundreds, of corpses in varying states of decay.

"It is a terrible sight, the stench is horrible. It's as if the bodies have been tortured. The dead have no dignity," she said in an interview with NBC after her photos became international news. "Our tradition says that after four days, the bodies of your loved ones should mix with the earth, otherwise how will their soul be released?" Dhun Baria's revelations led to a burial tradition stretching back thousands of years being challenged.

To compensate for the lack of vultures, the congregation had installed solar concentrators to speed up the decomposition. The leaders of the congregation had given assurances that this method would guarantee the effective disintegration of the bodies without breaking the many taboos related to contaminating the elements. When the sun shines, these panels enable the temperature to reach over 100°C (212°F), which cooks the bodies and contributes to their decomposition. But in Mumbai it is more often cloudy than sunny, and during the annual monsoon the solar concentrators are almost entirely ineffective.

CONSERVATIVE AND REFORMIST members of Mumbai's Parsi community have long debated the practice. The conservatives, who have had control over both the congregation and access to the holy places, have refused to give cremation and burial their approval. Congregation members who choose alternative burials will not have prayers read for them.

"For the Parsis in India, disposal of the dead has been a nightmarish problem," wrote one reader in 2010 in the magazine *Parsiana*, which in recent years has been dominated by the dispute between the various factions. Can electric cremations be a solution, or is electricity also a form of fire? Could the religion be dying out because more and more Parsis are renouncing its key dogmas, or because a group of conservative traditionalists is making it impossible for modern people to practice the religion?

In 2015, after many years of fighting to establish a crematorium in the Doongerwadi forest itself, a group of reformists opened a Parsi prayer room near a large crematorium in a different part of the city. The priests who took part in these ceremonies were immediately banned and accused of "blasphemous and irreligious activities." The reformists have long voiced concerns about what they call a "Talibanization" of the community, and saw the banning of the priests as yet another example of this.

It was not until the COVID-19 pandemic that there was even the slightest sign of agreement between the combatants. In 2020 the bodies of a number of orthodox Parsis who had died from COVID-19 were cremated by order of the authorities. After long and heated discussions within the community, it was decided that the deceased could still have prayers read for them in the temple. The religious dilemma finally had a practical solution.

9

A Monument to the Dead

From our little home office on the terrace, we have a view straight out towards the southern part of Oslo North Cemetery. Beyond the apple trees and the conifer hedge—where the city's drug addicts had a secluded picnic spot, until we moved into the house—we can just about see an elevation in the ground; a small hillock that looks deceptively similar to the burial mounds that have been found scattered throughout northern Europe since time immemorial. It looks like it was put there strategically, as the old Iron Age mounds were, at a suitable distance from the main building, and imposingly set in the landscape. Its shape is accentuated by five curved structures made of polished gray stone, which stretch the mound's length for several yards like elongated headstones. Up close you see that there are little plaques with names and dates attached to them. A monument to the dead, you realize, and in this case a memorial to people whose ashes have been scattered elsewhere or placed anonymously in an urn on the nearby lawn behind the bush.

The mound behind the house is used as a memorial garden. Recently, parallel with the rising numbers of the city's residents choosing cremation over burial, there has also been an increasing number of people wanting a memorial site for their loved ones, although not necessarily a separate grave. For many, a permanent grave with a headstone becomes more of a burden than a comfort;

a place that has to be visited regularly, maintained and cared for, planted and cleaned, a task that falls to the bereaved, regardless of where they live, or how interested they are in ornamental shrubs and candles on religious holidays. The thought of a rarely visited grave can become a constant source of guilt, weeds and dead plants an indication or accusation that the bereaved no longer care, just like the standard flowers the burials department put out, should you choose to pay for the service. In the aforementioned memorial garden, there are no such individual requirements. The deceased have name plaques, names beside names, all strangers who have nothing in common except the fact that they once existed. A public space for reflection instead of a private grave that you worry about neglecting. Between the stone structures there are spaces for candles and flowers which can be placed on three shared stands that are not connected to any specific plaque. So there are nearly always fresh flowers and candles burning. Around All Saints' Day and Christmas Eve, arcs of light rise from the mound.

The mound itself is nowhere near as old as it perhaps looks; it is not a memorial from the distant Iron Age. Nothing like it, in fact. During one of our graveyard strolls with erstwhile funeral director Stein Olav Hohle, we learn that the mound was built sometime in the mid-1970s as a creative answer to an urgent problem. The headstones from old, dismantled graves were piling up in the storage areas on the cemetery's far east side. No one quite knew what to do with them. Donating them for use as building material had a stigma attached, and past examples of the practice have almost exclusively negative connotations. The Nazis were known to use headstones from Jewish cemeteries to pave the streets, and more recently, in 2015, British property developer Kim Davies received a £60,000 fine and a significant dent in his reputation after using headstones from a children's cemetery to cover the decking at his house in Abergavenny, Wales. (The case gained extra notoriety because the house was known to have been where the popular children's hymn "All Things Bright and Beautiful" was written in the mid-1800s.)

At Oslo North Cemetery, an employee found a simple, inexpensive, and dignified way to solve the problem of the surplus headstones, and one spring day—probably in 1976—a large hole was dug, into which these headstones were themselves buried and covered with soil. It created a new feature in the landscape without any specific purpose. By doing this, the foundations for a new type of monument had been laid—perhaps without anyone fully appreciating the extent of the initiative. Several decades later, when the memorial garden was created, this "grave mound"—built using the remains of old graves—could now be used to commemorate new generations of dead.

While we assume that the Late Iron Age burial mounds were dedicated to individuals and significant figures that were well known in their lifetimes and probably for many years after, we can also assume that they served as a form of collective monument in their time. Our mound had been dug using an excavator and, originally, for no other reason than to solve a problem.

The construction of enormous, ancient tumuli must have kept whole communities busy with mound building for extended periods of time—sometimes for several months. A good example of this is the Oseberg burial mound, which gives us a sense of the different roles both individuals and the community played in the many rituals and activities that finally resulted in this highly symbolic visual demonstration of wealth, power, lineage, and veneration of the dead.

Oseberg, which was excavated in the summer of 1904 by archaeologists Gabriel Gustafson and Haakon Schetelig, is one of the world's most famous ship burials, alongside the slightly older Sutton Hoo burial in England. We know that the Oseberg ship was built from oak somewhere in western Norway, probably around the year 820, and may have been in normal service at sea for ten years before being hauled ashore for its final voyage. The burial chamber itself, which was on deck and behind the mast, was built from trees that were felled locally, in eastern Norway, in the summer of 834. So we know that it is highly likely the burial was carried out that year, or just a couple of years later. The ship was partially buried in airtight blue clay, and then covered with rocks, earth, and peat, so that the whole thing was almost hermetically sealed in the mound. When Gustafson and Schetelig unearthed the ship, the wood, metals, bones, and textiles were so well preserved that even today the entire ship and many of its objects can still be appreciated.

In connection with the burial chamber, the archaeologists found the skeletal remains of two women. What their relationship was in life is unclear, but it is believed that only one of them is the person for whom the grave was made. One of the women was significantly older than the other, possibly eighty years of age; the other must have been closer to fifty when she died. Recent examin-ations of the two skeletons confirm that both women had similar diets, at least during the years prior to their burial. They both ate well and had no obvious deficiencies in adulthood. However, the younger woman's DNA profile differs from that of the older one, and it would appear that she had roots in a different part of the world. Even though the various analyses point in slightly different direc-tions, there are indications she was originally from the area that is now Iran but was then ancient Persia. This might be surprising, but not improbable; we know that the Vikings traveled great distances both in the east and in the west. Many of the textiles found in the

Oseberg mound can also be linked to trade routes that already existed along the Silk Road. Perhaps the younger woman in the grave was one of the many people who were themselves sold as commodities? The older woman had advanced cancer and many skeletal injuries when she died. The younger woman's bones, however, reveal no injuries or trauma, other than a broken collarbone that had not fused completely. We cannot be sure that the women died at the same time, although since they were buried together it is likely that they did—or perhaps one had to die because the other one did. Both women seem to have been well treated in the final years of their lives; nevertheless, it is plausible that, if she came from another country, the younger woman was bound to the old woman in life, as a personal slave or servant, and therefore had to accompany the old woman in death. Of course, it could also have been the other way round, and the old woman had to follow an important woman in her prime to the grave.

Should you be predisposed to such things, for religious or cultural reasons, then another person's life and body could be considered the most exclusive gift you could take to your grave. There are many explanations for what grave gifts might have signified. Perhaps they were never intended as "gifts" at all—a tentatively more neutral term for the same thing is "grave goods," or "grave material." It is most likely that the objects we find in graves in different places and from different periods meant different things in their various contexts. It is possible that they were meant to represent the deceased, either as they were in life or in their new identity in death. Or it may have been that those left behind—close family members or powerful local figures—wanted themselves or others to be represented, to reflect their true position and strength, or the roles and social network that they *aspired* towards. We often imagine that the grave goods were meant to have a practical function—as a sacrifice, or to help and be used in the afterlife. But the accumulation of such enormous riches, like those found in the Oseberg ship, was clearly also a significant demonstration of power and status.

As mentioned in "Odin's Law," Snorri writes that "every man should come to Valhalla with such wealth as he had brought with him on the fire; what he had dug into the ground himself, he should also own." It is not clear what Odin thought about the women that were buried, but judging by the tomb of the Oseberg queen (as she is often referred to), we can assume that women of the elite at least were regarded similarly. In addition to the enormous ship—the oars, the anchor, the sail, and everything else that belongs to it—the two women (possibly only one of them, if we consider the other woman to be grave goods herself) had fifteen horses, two cows, six dogs, a beautifully carved full-size wagon, three magnificent chairs, two tents, six beds, and several other pieces of furniture, quilts and pillows, carpets, beautiful fabrics and dresses, five looms, a range of textile implements, masses of kitchen utensils, boxes and barrels of all sizes, baskets, buckets, bread, fruit and berries, five carved animal heads that have been interpreted as religious objects (and may have been carried in the funeral procession itself), several so-called "rattles" that were found with the animal heads, as well as combs, knives, shoes, glass beads, an embroidered tapestry illustrating what could be a funeral procession, and a small leather pouch containing cannabis. The burial chamber itself was comfortably furnished with a bed, bedsheets, feather duvets and pillows, clothing, and other exclusive textiles. The buckets of wild apples and blueberries were clearly fruits of the autumn harvest. However, buried under the blue clay, which had been excavated before the ship had been placed in the hole, were wildflowers typically found in spring and early summer. It is therefore assumed that at least four months elapsed from the time work on the mound began until the dead were finally placed in the grave. It also seems that the mound was closed in two different phases, so that for a while the ship remained partially exposed—perhaps so that it could be used as a stage on which the burial rituals could be performed?

Ibn Fadlan—the Arab chronicler who witnessed the burial of a Viking chief on the Volga in 922—writes that among the Rus a rich man's possessions were gathered and divided three ways upon his death. One third went to his family, another went towards making his burial clothes, and the final third went towards brewing the beer that would be drunk at his funeral. To give the bereaved enough time to make all the necessary preparations, the deceased man Fadlan wrote about was buried in a temporary grave for ten days.

Of course, much of what took place during those days on the Volga more than 1,000 years ago will never be found in the archaeo-logical material. Not least because the ship, containing the dead man, all his weapons, the slave girl, butchered and dismembered horses, and oxen, dogs, and chickens, was in the end burned instead of buried. Nevertheless, the descriptions of all the items placed in the grave with him, the tent that functioned as a burial cham-ber on the ship's deck, and the mound built over the site of the funeral pyre correspond so well with much of what was found in the Oseberg mound that it is tempting to imagine that even some of the rituals we cannot "see" would have been similar. As the English archaeologist Neil Price notes in his book *The Children of Ash and Elm* (2020), there are also parts of Fadlan's story where he seems to have been personally affected by some of the things he witnessed, descriptions that give his portrayals a greater degree of credibility than what you might otherwise suspect are the exaggerations or prejudices of a historian looking in from the outside. This specifically applies to the fate of one of the chief's slave women. Her story is one of the main reasons for the speculations about whether one of the two Oseberg women was a slave who was forced to (or wanted to?) follow her mistress to the grave.

When a chieftain dies, Fadlan explains, the slave girls are asked which of them wants to die with him. A straightforward question, seemingly based on the decision being voluntary, but it becomes clear that once you have stated your willingness to die you cannot change your mind. Two other slave girls are designated to look after and wait on the volunteering girl; washing her feet, singing with her, giving her delicious food to eat and as much beer as she can drink. On the day the dead chieftain is exhumed from his temporary grave, he is dressed in his new burial clothes before being placed in the tent on deck and supported by cushions and blankets. The corpse is tended to by an old woman—the "angel of death," as they call her—a dreadful-looking woman according to Fadlan. Throughout the morning, animals are slaughtered and tossed into the ship. The horses are chased around until they are drenched in sweat, then killed and chopped into pieces. While this is happening, the slave girl goes from tent to tent to have sex with all the chief's men. In the afternoon the girl is taken to a wooden frame, a kind of "door frame," over which she is lifted—three times—while proclaiming that she can see all her loved ones in the afterlife, including the chief himself. They are waiting for her.

Finally, the girl is taken aboard the ship, where she is given beer to drink before her last farewell. She drags the proceedings out, Fadlan writes, but the "angel of death," who is standing beside the girl, nags her to hurry up and finish the drink: "When I looked at her she looked completely bewildered." Then the old woman forces the slave girl into the tent. The men standing around them have wooden sticks which they start beating on their shields, to drown out the slave girl's screams, we are told, to avoid frightening the other girls from volunteering next time someone important dies. Six men then follow the two women into the tent where, beside the corpse, they take turns raping the young woman before helping the old woman strangle and stab her to death.

Blood all over the place, sweat, the smell of sex, mortal terror, agonized screams, beer and more beer, singing and pounding rhythms. We will probably never know if that is exactly what happened at Oseberg, but there is no doubt that to many people these funerals would have been a dramatic, perhaps gruesome, and highly sensory event. The remaining monument was for a long time a testimony to this, a kind of physical memory—first of known members of the family and the local community, and eventually of ancestors who connected new generations to the landscape and an increasingly mythical past.

A recent study and comparison of the monumental ship graves found in East Anglia as well as in western and eastern Norway highlight the mythological ancestral motif in trying to explain the origin of the ship symbolism in this funerary tradition. Although the ship burials at Snape and Sutton Hoo are earlier (dated from the late sixth to early seventh centuries) than any of the known Viking ship burials in Norway, the characteristics that make Sutton Hoo unique in a British context show clear impulses from earlier and contemporary Scandinavian ship settings (giant structures made of stone), boat graves (which are smaller than the ship graves), and mounds. The inspiration behind the constructions of monumental ship graves might, however, according to archaeologist Jan Bill, be found in the English national epos Beowulf. The poem originates from a long oral tradition with links back to Migration Period Scandinavia, composed possibly around the late 7th century, but preserved in a manuscript from about 1000 CE. In the prologue, we read the evocative legend of the mythical Danish king Scyld, who is said to have come to his people as a small child in a drifting boat and, upon his death, was sent off again by means of a ship funeral. The legend serves as an example of a certain type of old origin myth that Bill argues ascendant royal families would have been likely to evoke to legitimize their own power. "The majority of monumental burials using the ship allegory," he concludes, can thus be interpreted as "manifestations" of such a ruling-class ideology, and to have been "created to establish the godly origin of a deceased dynastic head in collective memory, thereby ensuring the transfer of this exclusive status to his or her heirs."

The Oseberg ship and Sutton Hoo are among the most famous north European burial mounds—a part of the world's heritage and evidence of the rocky north's rich and vibrant culture. But they seem small and quite modest when compared to Egypt's pyramids, the biggest and most famous of the world's many death monuments. The Pyramid of Khufu at Giza (also known as the Pyramid of Cheops, according to Greek historians) was initially 480 feet (146 m) high at its tallest point, with an area or footprint of over 62,000 square yards (52,000 sq. m). It is the largest, by volume, of all the Egyptian pyramids, and were it situated next to the memorial garden outside our window, rather than in the desert outside Cairo, it would have towered over all of the other buildings and the surrounding city, covering 30 percent of the cemetery. The Pyramids of Giza were built between 2686 and 2181 BCE during what is referred to as the Old Kingdom, a period of relative stability in the succession of various dynasties and their pharaohs. They represent the pinnacle of grand funerary monuments and memorials erected for rulers who were not only kings on earth but worshipped as gods after their death.

So far more than a hundred pyramids have been found in total, on the various pyramid fields of Egypt and Sudan to the west of the River Nile. But pyramids did not just come out of nowhere. The first examples of the Egyptians' distinctive worshipping of the dead are the mastabas: rectangular funerary monuments that were originally built for kings hundreds of years before the first pyramids, and continued to be built alongside the pyramids hundreds of years after their arrival—first for kings, but eventually for prominent members of the court and officials. They were smaller than the pyramids, of course, which probably explains why they are far less well known, but they are equally impressive. These rectangular buildings could be 10 meters tall and cover an area greater than 1,200 square yards (1,000 sq. m). The mastabas were built from mud bricks, which consisted of sand and clay extracted from the delta, and were oriented north to south, a common feature of all Egypt's burial chambers that was continued with the tombs inside the otherwise square pyramids. The tombs inside the pyramids of Giza have a deviation of less than 0.05 percent from this north–south axis, a level of precision that has puzzled and fascinated scientists for almost a century.

After all, while the pyramids were relatively rare honors dedicated to the few, there were hundreds of mastabas, with more than 150 of them on the Giza plateau alone. Each mastaba would often include a reception room, a chapel, and a room for offerings, while the burial chamber itself would be dug into the bedrock and protected by an intricate system of hidden doors, pitfalls, and curses. Another name for mastaba is the hard-to-pronounce and vowelless ancient Egyptian word *pr-dtj*, which directly translated means something close to "house of eternity."

The search for eternal life was central to the ancient Egyptians' willingness to use huge amounts of resources on grand funerals, impressive "houses of eternity" for their dead, and not least the deliberate preservation of corpses. The practice of mummification began shortly after King Djoser's architect constructed the very first pyramid around 2670 BCE. By building six mastabas of decreasing size on top of each other, he created a so-called step pyramid, approximately 200 feet (60 m) tall.

Egypt was one of the wealthiest states of its time, an advanced agricultural society that was also heavily involved in production and trade. But you might ask what consequences using resources on funerary monuments had on the development of the country. If you consider the basic principle of the modern economy, the fuel for eternal growth—that profits from trade and production should be reinvested—it seems almost perverse that they allowed such enormous sums to be spent on huge symbolic buildings way out in the desert. Did they deliberately squander large parts of the state coffers? All of the resources that went into these tombs—not just the king's resources but anyone rich enough to crave immortality—would have to have been paid for somehow.

The Egyptians' extravagant mortuary practices are frequently cited as an example of the staggering wastefulness often found in authoritarian theocracies with their god-kings and priestly rule. Others claim, however, that these constructions were not necessarily any different to similar projects built today, like bridges in sparsely populated areas, landmark buildings, and arts centers. As well as fulfilling the obvious role of underlining the regime's power and the promise of eternal life, these funerary monuments were also infrastructure projects that stimulated the economy. Recent archaeological investigations on the outskirts of the large necropolises connected to the pyramids and mastabas have revealed what have been interpreted as living areas for the builders. It was previously thought that the laborers who built the pyramids had to be slaves drawn from a cowed population, but there is plenty of evidence that these construction sites were too extensive for that to be the case. There were also numerous architects, engineers, stonemasons, porters, animal handlers, clerks, middle management, cooks, and bakers, all working with pride and dignity and financially compensated.

However, by antiquity it was also clear that these enormous complexes attracted grave robbers. Despite the secret passageways and elaborate methods used to hide and secure the tombs, few of the mummies from the great pyramids appear to have escaped the robbers' hands. This looting risk could well be the main reason the pyramids stopped being built. During the New Kingdom—the period between 1550 and 1069 BCE, famous for its well-preserved mummies and not least Tutankhamun's fabulous tomb—kings were buried in the Valley of the Kings, in secret burial chambers carved into the mountainside. But even these tombs were not safe from thieves and vandals. In fact, the tomb of Tutankhamun is one of the very few tombs to have been found more or less intact—the reason we today know in detail about the vast riches that were intended to accompany Tutankhamun in the afterlife.

IT IS ALSO relatively common to find looters' pits in Iron Age burial mounds. When the burial ground at Gulli—not far from the Oseberg mound—was studied in the early 2000s, seven of the twenty graves that were preserved and could be examined in detail were found to have been reopened fairly soon after the burial event. Correspondingly, only eight of the graves had definitely not been looted.

A common explanation for this kind of activity has been that people simply wanted the goods and gold they contained. Today, most archaeologists believe that the plundering may also have had entirely different motives, and that these incidents may have been part of longer processes in society at large, in which the mounds, as monuments and memorials, played a crucial role. In several places, it is believed that a mound burial may have been reserved for one person per generation, and that the mounds therefore were associated with lineage, ownership, and rights to the land and estate. That a new chief and clan could consolidate their position socially and politically by destroying, or in other ways making use of, the graves of previous rulers in the area is therefore a possible explanation.

The Oseberg mound also has clear signs of looting. Among the grave goods, the mound also contained eighteen shovels, some of which have been dated to roughly 120 years after the actual grave. In other words, many of the spades appear to have belonged to the grave robbers, and the archaeologists who dated the spades believe these dates coincide with Harald "Bluetooth" Gormsson's rise to power and dominance in neighboring Denmark and east Norway. Perhaps the Oseberg queen's legacy was pillaged by the Danish king's supporters?

Other possible interpretations for some of the looting can perhaps be linked more directly to the actual grave goods. Not necessarily to the luxury and economic values, but to the way things and objects can be given "new life" in new contexts.

A strange absence among the wealth of riches and material items that the grave robbers left in the Oseberg mound is the jewelry. Normally the most common grave goods found in Viking Age women's graves are pairs of oval brooches, fastened parallel to the chest and often joined by a string of beads—a jewelry set that appears to have been a standard part of women's dress at the time.

Why did neither of the two women buried in the Oseberg mound have personal ornaments with them? Like so many other cases where archaeology gives us a mere fragment of prehistory, we can only guess. But we do know that grave robbers must have entered the tomb itself and rummaged around. The skeletal remains of the elderly woman were found by the archaeologists in the plunder shaft—that is, the tunnel that the robbers had dug to gain access to the grave. She must have been dragged from the bed she was lying on and out of the chamber, presumably while her body was still partially intact. Maybe the robbers took the jewelry before fleeing (they had clearly abandoned the shovels in a hurry)—the pieces were small and far easier to carry than many of the other items. Maybe the personal ornaments were the reason for the looting in the first place; that there was a deliberate plan for what would be taken from the grave, and what would be left behind?

If we remember the Iron Age blacksmith and his possible role as a ritual specialist, it is even possible to imagine that in some cases the looters might have been looking for bones, in order to forge the deceased's personal qualities into a new sword blade, or a piece of beautiful jewelry. It is also possible to imagine that when objects were buried with important members of the family or an important chieftain, they may have acquired a new or different meaning after a certain number of years in the mound, or after a special occasion involving the remaining family. Perhaps, by being reintroduced into society, these objects could regain an important role among the living.

AT OUR LOCAL cemetery there are neither kings nor queens. There are, however, many ordinary people, all buried in a quite ordinary cemetery in accordance with modern Scandinavian tradition. Even the "burial mound"—as we have now learned—is a shared monument commemorating the many. The cemetery is otherwise located as a demilitarized zone of consecrated land in a city that was, until recently, strictly divided by class, between the bourgeoisie's self-owned gardens in the north and west, the urban bourgeoisie in the south, and the working-class districts in the east. Throughout its 130 years, the cemetery has been used almost exclusively by the eastern neighborhoods. While the more prestigious Cemetery of Our Saviour is full of distinguished titles like Merchant, Director, Cavalry Master, and Tobacco Manufacturer, many of the titles on the headstones at Oslo North Cemetery attest to classic working-class occupations interspersed with humble clerks and civil servants like tram conductors, teachers, and trade union representatives. It is no coincidence that the memorial to the members of Norway's Communist Party who were killed in the Second World War was erected here.

But not everyone is the same. The Martinsen family were the owners of the local flour mill, one of the industrial enterprises along Oslo's Aker River. Unlike many of the factory owners, who lived in more upmarket areas, the mill's founder, Gustav Martinsen, chose to settle near the factory, in an elegant director's villa that lacked nothing, in stark contrast to the nearby workers' houses. The family also bought a grave plot, which, if possible, contrasted even more starkly with its surroundings. At the cemetery's highest point, they built a memorial with a 13-foot-high (4 m) sculpture by the artist Lars Utne depicting a grieving woman. In the sculpture's base there is a black door with a metal grill, through which you can see a staircase leading down to a crypt, and on top of the solid foundation around the sculpture and crypt there is a beautifully decorated metal lid, engraved with the names of those buried inside. The grave is still in use, and the last inscriptions are from well into the 2000s. For today's casual passers-by, the monument perhaps appears more like a memorial to a time when some people were remembered more than others.

Displaying one's status in death is no longer commonplace in most of Western society. It not only conflicts with the idea that we should be equal in death, in Norway it is also against the law. Today's gravestones are allowed to be a maximum height of 5 feet (1.5 m), and a maximum width of 2 feet (0.6 m) for single graves and 4 feet (1.2 m) for family graves. The Martinsen family are one of the last generations who could continue showing how prosperous they were in death. Having said that, of course, despite today's regulations and the modern ideas of equality, not *everyone* has to choose a headstone that fits within the modest dimensions of a few inches.

There are still exceptions for certain notabilities. Just outside Hollywood, in Glendale, California, celebrities from the world of entertainment—including Walt Disney, Humphrey Bogart, Liberace, and Michael Jackson (in a tomb that is supposedly empty)—are, in death, allowed to play the role of modern-day royalty at Forest Lawn Memorial Park, a cemetery with all the trappings of a blockbuster production, complete with replicas of Michelangelo's *David* and Leonardo's *Last Supper*.

Neither do genuine members of royalty appear to have any ideals of modesty in death, as seen in the anything-but-modest funeral of Queen Elizabeth II in 2022. In Denmark, too—where the royal family's unbroken lineage stretches back to the Middle Ages—38 former regents are buried in Roskilde Cathedral. Queen

Margrethe II, herself a trained archaeologist and artist, has been in close dialogue with the artist who in 2003 began designing the funerary monument for her and her husband, Prince Henrik. In 2018 the sarcophagus stood finished in Sankta Birgitta's chapel, temporarily covered in anticipation of its future occupant. The sarcophagus is made of cast glass in which two sandblasted figures, representing the queen and her prince consort, can be seen. However, as early as 2017 it became known that the Danish prince— who had long expressed his frustration at not being given the title of king—had no intention of being buried with his wife. The then head of communications for the Danish royal family confirmed to the Danish media that this was a "natural consequence of the fact that he has not been treated equally, in relation to his spouse, by being denied the title and function he wanted." When Prince Henrik died in February 2018, he was cremated and his ashes scattered, partly on the sea and partly in the gardens of Fredensborg Palace. The prince had refused to follow the queen into the grave. Despite the many years of preparation, when the time comes, this queen will be buried alone.

10

The Empty and Nameless Grave

Compared to the size of the overall population, very few people simply vanish. Of those that do go missing, most reappear after a short time. But on rare occasions, the person's disappearance will be due to a tragic incident or crime, and those who *are* found will no longer be alive. This is what happened in the case of Jeanette, who went missing in October 2017. Jeanette was a young woman with a troubled past. She was known to often withdraw and go under the radar for short periods, but when Christmas approached and her family did not hear from her, they became worried and reported her missing. They inquired around the places she frequented and spoke to friends and acquaintances, and when that yielded no results, they handed out leaflets, hung up posters, and involved journalists and public agencies. They feared the worst, and in doing so experienced a distinct form of grief which the head of the police's missing-persons bureau, Anders Oksvold, in one of several national newspaper articles about the Jeanette case, called "waiting grief." Absence and grief without closure.

When Jeanette was finally found in the summer of 2020, she was dead. It turned out that she had been dead for a long time, and more than that, she had already been laid to rest at the Cemetery of Our Saviours in Oslo. But she was not among the other graves. Her body was found in a manhole beneath one of the cemetery's paths. For almost three years, visitors and cemetery staff had passed over the manhole cover, unaware of what was lying beneath. A cunning place to hide the evidence of a murder, you might think. Who would ever search for a corpse in a cemetery?

No one knows how much longer Jeanette's body would have lain there, had the man who put her there not reported the whole thing to the police himself.

It should, by the way, be pointed out that this man—who held the key to solving this missing-person case—is not and never has been suspected of having taken the woman's life. When he met Jeanette on the street by chance, in autumn 2017, they were old acquaintances within Oslo's drug scene. They had seen each other and waved several times in recent years. He told a newspaper that he had helped her because he thought she was a "nice, kind girl who had ended up on heroin," whom he had wanted to look after—without there being any relationship between them. On this occasion she was especially tired and run-down, and he invited her to his apartment to rest. He gave her a cheese sandwich, which she ate before going to sleep, and then the man went out for a walk. When he returned to his apartment later that day, he found Jeanette dead on the sofa.

At the time, he already had a prior conviction which he was about to serve time for; his life was a mess, his nerves frayed, and so he panicked. Instead of contacting the police, with all the unpleasantness that would entail, he decided to hide the body. But where can you hide a corpse? Engulfed by the current chaos, between the shock of finding Jeanette dead, his fear of the police, and the consequences of being found with a dead body, the man wanted to give the woman a dignified resting place. So he chose the cemetery. It was an extremely improvised grave, but still within an area where people can rest in peace.

In prison, however, his conscience gnawed at him when he thought about Jeanette's family, who were still looking for their girl and would never have peace without knowing what had happened to her. So in the summer of 2020, he contacted the police, and Jeanette was found. The parents would now have a grave they could visit.

Just the knowledge that there is a grave to visit can help many with their grieving. The grave is a specific place, a physical monument and gathering point for the bereaved. It is an important part of the grieving process. This also applies when those presumed deceased are *not* found, those lost in missing-persons cases, after natural disasters, accidents at sea, and during wars or other dramatic or devastating events. It could be a sunken ship, someone who vanished in the mountains or while traveling in a remote area, a missing dementia patient or person who is suspected of being suicidal—sometimes it will be the disappearance of a child. But after the search operations and the months or years of uncertainty, a missing person will be declared dead.

In most countries today, graves are permitted even when the body is missing. The technical term for such a grave accurately describes its function—*cenotaph*, which is derived from the Greek words *kenos* and *taphos* for "empty tomb." A place to remember and honor the dead who never came home.

Among the many variations in burial practices that we are aware of from the Nordic Iron Age, we also know of surprisingly many graves that do not contain bodies. Whether we can really determine if they were constructed as graves, or cenotaphs, is a timely question. It can be hard to establish why actions were taken and installations built hundreds or thousands of years ago.

In Gunnarstorp in southeastern Norway, however, there is a burial ground that is so interesting for its *lack* of bodies that it demands closer inspection. The oldest graves here, from the Late Bronze Age, are more than 3,000 years old. Otherwise, most are from the Early Iron Age, from about 500 BCE to about 400 CE. When the site was excavated decades ago the archaeologists found 153 flat stone settings that were all thought to be graves. Most of these constructions were round or oval, but some were triangular, square, or of an otherwise indeterminate shape. As expected, many of the stone settings also contained burned human bones—the remains of the cremation practiced at the time—totally in line with the assumption that the stone structures were graves. The surprising thing was that more than half of these graves contained no human remains at all. Nothing about the graves themselves, neither their shape nor their location, suggests there is any difference between those *with* and those *without* human remains. They are spread across the burial ground and seem to have been similarly designed. They did not contain many grave goods, but those that were found—mostly ceramics and a few other objects—seem to have been distributed between the various plots regardless of whether they were occupied graves or cenotaphs. Just as an empty grave with a headstone in a modern-day cemetery would look no different from any other grave—whether it contained ashes or a coffin—it seems like the graves at Gunnarstorp could not be identified as one or the other based on their above-ground characteristics. So we might consider it quite likely that they were all intended to be memorials, as in a large number of empty graves, in a relatively small area, over many generations. But what had happened to the dead?

One possible explanation could be found at Alken Enge, outside Illerup in Denmark, where, if we remember, several hundred warriors were found in a mass grave dating from the period when the graves and cenotaphs of Gunnarstorp were in use. There is no reason to believe that these warriors actually came from Gunnarstorp, but they remind us how much society during the Iron Age was characterized by violence, warlike behavior, and the displacement of people over relatively large distances. That people did not always come home was probably expected during several periods and across many places. Those who perished at Alken Enge received no proper burial from their executioners, they were just left in the open and then thrown into the lake. Nevertheless, perhaps they were commemorated somewhere entirely different, in a place such as at Gunnarstorp. It would be consistent with numerous other mortuary practices: we honor our own, and discard our enemies, consigning them to an unmarked grave.

There are many known Viking Age memorials to the fallen dead who never came home. Thousands of rune stones were engraved and erected in prominent locations, at crossroads, fords, or on small hills. The earliest known examples date back to the fifth century, and it was a practice that continued well into the Christian era (most rune stones are located in Sweden and date back to the eleventh century). The runes were engraved by skilled specialists, masters of the art, and whoever had the means and the power to commission these monuments must have come from the elite layer of society. The inscriptions often list the name of the person who commissioned the runes, who the stone was raised in memory of, and sometimes even the name of the rune maker. The vast majority of stones were raised in memory of a deceased individual, woman or man, often, it is believed, as a way of "documenting" family relationships, land affiliation, and inheritance rights. Now and then, however, we also find inscriptions bearing witness to the fate and exploits of individuals. In central Sweden, more than thirty rune stones have been found that seemingly commemorate the same historical event, referencing the men who died "in Austerled, with Ingvar."

Ingvar the Far-Traveled was a Swedish chieftain who led an impressive campaign eastwards from 1036 to 1042, and who had his own saga written about him. Like so much of the Norse saga literature, separating myth from reality is not always easy. However, it would appear that Ingvar was a successful young man who in 1036 sailed east along the Volga, all the way down to the Caspian Sea, and maybe even further. He led a large fleet comprising several ships and many men, most of them presumably from the same area around Mälaren in which most of the so-called Ingvar stones have been found. Ingvar, and most of his crew, died in the east and never came home.

No stone has ever been found for Ingvar himself, but his half-brother Harald was given one of the most famous:

Tola let ræisa stæin þennsa at sun sinn Harald, broður Ingvars.
Þæiʀ foru drængila fiarri at gulli
ok austarla ærni gafu,
dou sunnarla a Særklandi.

Tóla had this stone raised in memory of her son Harald,
    Ingvar's brother.
They traveled valiantly far for gold,
and in the east gave (food) to the eagle.
(They) died in the south in Serkland.

Observant readers may be tempted to think that Harald and his brother became food for the eagle, just as in the sky burials that were practiced for millennia in the Far East. However, "giving food to the eagle" is a familiar expression often found in Old Norse poetry and saga literature; a poetic way of saying "killing one's enemies." So it was Harald and Ingvar's enemies who became food for the eagle on the battlefield, albeit without the sacred rituals or tower of silence. Where and how Ingvar's men were buried over there in Serkland is impossible to know today. No "typical" Viking graves have been found that far east.

In Europe, however, several recent discoveries of mass graves can be linked specifically to Viking raids, where comrades in arms of Scandinavian origin have been buried together. Two of these cases testify, on the one hand, to the warriors' solidarity and how they cared for each other when a proper burial was possible, and on the other hand, to the hatred and thirst for revenge among the people who suffered their attacks.

In 2008 and 2012, two so-called boat graves were discovered and excavated on the Estonian island of Saaremaa. Both ships, one a long rowboat, the other a large ship, were filled with dead warriors. Altogether there were at least 41 men, all in their prime, most of them in their thirties. Seven of them were found in the rowboat, sitting upright by the oars. The other 34 lay neatly beside each other, in four layers, at the bottom of the ship's hull. Many of the skeletons are marked by signs of battle and violent deaths, involving injuries from cuts, blows, and arrowheads. The men took their weapons to the grave, along with piles of food and a couple of birds of prey. Pieces from a strategy game, a kind of "Viking chess," were also strewn over the corpses. The "king" piece had been placed in the mouth of the individual lying in the middle—once clearly a high-ranking man, as we can see from the ring sword he was buried with. The men's shields had been lain on top of them, forming a kind of protective roof, and on top of that a large piece of cloth:

the sail of the ship. It is a moving example of tenderness—if we can allow ourselves to use such an expression for people who were obviously mass murderers.

The ships on Saaremaa are for several reasons considered unique archaeological discoveries. Their ages are particularly interesting since the ships date back to around 750 CE, which is several decades before the first written sources mention the Viking raids—the attack on Lindisfarne monastery in 793 CE, for example, is normally considered the beginning of the Viking Age. So the Vikings had traveled east long before we find them in the Anglo-Saxon chronicles. It is also interesting to speculate as to who buried all these men. The parallels to the Scandinavian tradition of boat—and eventually ship—burials are obvious, even if there are no other known mass graves that included boats. The level of care and diligence that went into the burial, at least, lends weight to the assumption that it was the deceased's friends who made sure they had a decent final journey. It should also allow us to assume that the event that led to all these deaths—the raid, the battle, or whatever it was—was ultimately won by the Scandinavians.

The second mass grave bears testament to something quite different. It dates back to the latter part of the Viking Age, more than two hundred years after the Saaremaa ships. In Dorset, England, sometime between 970 and 1025 CE, about fifty young men were stripped naked, beheaded, and dumped in an old quarry. Their heads had been piled up in a corner of the grave, but some appeared to be missing. Perhaps they had been mounted on stakes, or kept by others for reasons that would be considered grotesque to us today? The corpses otherwise lay in a chaotic and disorderly manner. Items that would have been a normal part of their attire, such as brooches, buttons, and belt buckles, were missing. All their clothing and personal equipment had been removed by whoever put them in their grave. Several of the men seem to have attempted to defend themselves and had injuries to their hands and arms. Their slayers clearly had problems too—or were not particularly careful—when decapitating the men. Injuries on the skeletons show that each individual received an average of four cuts aimed at the head, shoulders, and neck before the head was finally detached from the body. In other words, it was pure execution, carried out with sluggish, brutal thoroughness. DNA and isotope analyses of teeth and bones show that the men came from Scandinavia and subarctic regions.

Many of them had clearly done a lot of travelling in the Nordic regions during their lives. But how they ended up in Dorset, like this, is more difficult to say. The men were young and, unlike the experienced warriors on Saaremaa, do not appear to have had previous battle injuries. Were they inexperienced raiders who had, a little too boldly, set off on their quest? Had they walked into a trap? Or were they young men from a settled Norse population who were executed to avenge the atrocities of other Vikings? What we can be sure of, at least, is that they received very little honor in death.

Whatever explanatory models we support, there is no doubt that the warriors buried in Dorset had a similar fate to others who ended up in mass graves, whether we are talking about the victims of the Black Death lying in plague pits or the outright genocides that have been committed in our own time. The stigma of the mass grave is linked to a fear of losing control. It is a loss that leaves us unable to bury our dead in the manner we would most prefer, and awakens our fear of humankind's underlying brutality. The cruelties of life, war, and violence are sometimes continued by willfully depriving a person of their dignity in death. Today we are familiar with a soldier's fear of leaving fallen comrades on the battlefield—it has been an often-depicted subject in popular culture, and the basis for planned and dangerous military operations.

IN 1994, RWANDA's slowly escalating civil war suddenly exploded when the country's president was assassinated. For three months, the country was engulfed by a chaotic and—as later became known—carefully planned bloodbath. Observers from the United Nations—and anyone else from the international community who could—left the country. No one knew what was happening, but you could get an indication from the rivers that flowed out of the country, which were brimming with human corpses, in some places thousands per day. In a few short months, from April to July, extremists from the country's Hutu majority carried out a genocide in which almost a million people were killed. Most of the dead belonged to the country's Tutsi minority, but many of them were Hutus considered disloyal to the extremists' genocidal program. The dead also included a large proportion of the country's already extremely vulnerable Twa pygmies.

One of the numerous massacres that took place happened in the church at Ntarama about 20 miles (32 km) from the capital, Kigali. When the unrest erupted, thousands of people sought refuge in the church, which they had been told was a safe place. But that was far from the case. The church was collaborating with the regime, and in many places the priests were conspiring with the killers themselves. Terrified families waited for two days before the army arrived, but instead of protecting the civilians from the local militias, the soldiers opened fire. When a hole was smashed into the church wall so they could shoot inside, the bodies toppled out on top of each other.

Several months later, when Andreas visited the country on a reporting trip, Rwanda was still in a state of paralysis. The cleanup had not properly started, and in Ntarama, the corpses were still lying where they had fallen. After the flies had done their work, white bones lay shining in the sun, in some places you could see the bullet holes in the skulls, while nylon dresses and suits, patches of hair, and children's plastic shoes lay seemingly untouched by the passing of time. Hanging beside the pulpit was a list of hymns that were sung at the last regular service, and there were children's drawings on the wall. Death was everywhere in Ntarama in 1995—in the scattered bones and teeth, in the toys and books, in the remains of the fearful crowding, in the intense and unbearable smell. And in the truly horrifying realization that the crunch beneath your feet, as you walk along a path, is exactly what you think it is: a now unidentifiable part of what was once a human.

Since July 1994, the Rwandan government has been based on the group who were victims of the genocide, the Tutsi-dominated Rwandan Patriotic Front, a de facto one-party government whose primary stated goal is that the genocide—which was by no means the country's first—should never be repeated. This government represented those who died, in the church in Ntarama, and in the many other churches, schools, hospitals, and community centers around the country. It was *their* dead.

The cleaning-up task in the months after the genocide was enormous. Rwanda was a place where every road sign had bullet holes, hardly a door was intact, every house had been ransacked, every closed door blasted open. The country's entire infrastructure had collapsed. When the time came and one could devote oneself to the church in Ntarama, the authorities made a radical choice: instead of burying the dead, the Rwandan government chose to

preserve Ntarama, turning the mass grave into a national monument—along with five other similar national memorials. Rwanda
has attempted to erase the shame from death by allowing the place
where these people died to become a kind of modern shrine, a
testimony, and a warning to the world. Ntarama's derelict church
has been given an extra roof, but remains otherwise as it was, with
broken windows and, in the wall near the pulpit, the hole that the
soldiers smashed in using sledgehammers before poking their
machine guns through.

The death tolls at these places are staggering. At the largest
memorial, in Kigali, lie the remains of 250,000 people who were
killed during the months of bloodshed. At a similar memorial
center in Nyamata, 20 miles (32 km) further south, there are more
than 45,000. In order for the site to be about more than breath-
taking numbers, the Nyamata Center's architects created a kind
of installation to illustrate how these staggering death statistics
concern individuals, each and every one of them: in a grave, or well,
decorated with white tiles, is the white-clad coffin of 32-year-old
Annonciata Mukandoli, who was one of those raped and killed
by Nyamata's local militia. Above the well, a glass shelf contains
dozens of skulls belonging to some of the thousands of others who
died here on April 13 and 14, 1994. The mass grave has become a
conscious choice. It is considered the most important and dignified
way of remembering the catastrophe that made it necessary, and of
honoring its victims.

AN UNMARKED GRAVE has long been the symbol of disaster, or
poverty and unknown status, which is why remembering the individuals among Rwanda's staggering death toll is so important. It
is also why, in most countries today, even those who die without

friends and relatives are given a funeral ceremony, often arranged by the authorities in near-empty rooms.

This loneliness is also evident at Oslo North Cemetery. We did not know at the time, but our search for an opening in the fence while trying to reach the maternity ward in the hours before welcoming our youngest son into the world had taken us through an area previously reserved for paupers' graves. In daylight it is still possible to see that there is something special here. While the headstones in the surrounding plots are laid out in even rows, in only slight variations of gray stone, and with almost the same height and appearance, the paupers' graves are more loosely distributed. The place looks unused and empty. But it is not.

Those buried here were those who, for one reason or another, had no family willing or able to pay for the funeral, and so instead received a simple burial at the municipality's expense—"on behalf of friends." These graves, for which the municipality are responsible, were given just a simple marker, usually a white wooden cross. When these crosses toppled or went rotten, after a harsh winter or at best after several years, they were removed and the area was again left open, like a meadow, despite the fact that the grave's interment period still applied as usual. Some families have subsequently chosen to erect headstones, but there are still no more than twelve of them in an area that would normally accommodate close to 150. One of these headstones is shaped like a Russian Orthodox cross with Cyrillic letters. A few of them are recent, and some of the graves have clearly been reopened for further use. Otherwise, those resting here are nameless, gone forever.

Paupers' graves still exist, but they are now placed between the other graves in the cemetery rather than in a designated section of their own. Much of the stigma around them is therefore gone.

However, the most remarkable thing about the old "paupers' section" is not those who were buried at the municipality's expense, but a part of the burial practice that is not written in any regulations or ordinances: in addition to the paupers' graves, the area was also used as a place to bury infants. They could be unborn babies that died late in pregnancy, who, for various reasons, were not sent to the hospital incinerator, or infants who were stillborn or died during childbirth. Even live-born babies who died within the first few days of their lives would end up here.

We are used to the dead being buried, one by one, shortly after their deaths. The corpses of these children received no such individual treatment, says a former employee of Oslo's burials authority, who, decades later, is still upset about these burials. Children's dead bodies were kept in a hospital cold room, and when a pauper's grave was about to be used—that is, when an adult individual was about to be buried—the children would be buried along with the deceased adult. Burials in paupers' graves did not happen often, so it could be months, sometimes as long as six months, before the children's bodies were interred. There could be as many as ten or fifteen child corpses in the grave with the adult. Alan the alcoholic, surrounded by a dozen children's corpses. The children did not get a coffin; instead, they would be placed in a simple cardboard box or wrapped in a blanket. Sometimes it would just be paper. What would an archaeologist make of our society and burial customs if they found a grave like this without knowing any of the context?

"The mothers were just told to go home and try again," says the former employee of the funeral authority. "Afterwards, many of them came to us asking where their children were buried. But there was a limit to how much we could help them. The grave belonged to the adult, so we were not allowed to say which grave it was. We could only tell them in which area it was located. The mothers despaired, and it was painful for us to see their despair." Today, the practice of burying stillborn babies in mass graves has long been a thing of the past, and separate children's memorial gardens have been established in several of our local cemeteries. These places are surrounded by flowering trees in spring, inspired by the Cherry Valley in Astrid Lindgren's book *The Brothers Lionheart* (1973).

MASS GRAVES NEVER cease to be upsetting. We saw this clearly among the U.S. population in April 2020, when, a few months after the world began realizing that we were in the midst of a global pandemic, a series of drone photos of Hart Island, just outside New York's Bronx borough, were published. The photos showed men in white hazmat suits stacking simple pine coffins on top of each other and side by side in long, deep ditches that looked like trenches. The scenes were reminiscent of medieval plague pits, and of wars and genocides in totally different parts of the world. What was going on? Why was the city burying its dead in mass graves? Hart Island's mass graves became emblematic of a system that had collapsed. A civilized country—the world's richest, no less—that was no longer able to care for its dead.

The truth is more complicated. Since 1869, Hart Island has been used as New York's city cemetery, or Potter's Field, as it is colloquially known. According to the New York City Council's website, it is the largest tax-funded cemetery in the world. More than a million people have been buried here over the years—a fact that has led others to refer to the island as the biggest mass grave in the world. In a country where funerals have become commercialized, expensive, and dependent on a certain amount of financial success, Potter's

Field on Hart Island is still associated with loneliness, poverty, and shame.

"Potter's field" is an often-used term in English-speaking countries for cemeteries reserved for poor people, unidentified corpses, and the deceased whose family or friends never collected them for burial. It also has an unpleasant etymological origin, from one of the Bible's numerous gloomy moments. Before Judas kills himself in remorse for betraying Jesus, he throws the silver coins he received for his betrayal into the temple. The priests inside pick up the money (they seem quite unmoved by the incident otherwise: "'What do we care?' they replied"), but they do not want to put the "blood money" in the temple coffers. They instead "took counsel and bought with them the potter's field as a burial place for strangers. Therefore that field has been called the Field of Blood to this day."

In New York's Field of Blood, coffins were seen piled up, three high, two wide, and in rows of 25—perhaps more if the coffins were small—before the ditch they had been placed in was covered with soil and a single, numbered, concrete block put up to mark the spot. No names, nothing to identify the dead lying in this common grave full of other unknowns. Many saw this as a clear picture of the sort of consequences a free-flowing pandemic can have in such a metropolis, where people live in close proximity and have no way of protecting themselves from the infection. So it was perhaps also surprising when subsequent news reports made it clear that this was not some unusual practice due to overcrowded morgues caused by COVID-19. On the contrary, it was how people—around eight hundred a year during the 2000s—had been buried on Hart Island the entire time the island had been the "city's cemetery."

The work of digging trenches and stacking corpses is done by inmates from the prison on the neighboring island, who work four days a week for 50 cents an hour. Public access is currently only available by ferry, which goes to the island twice a month. The cemetery is administered by New York's Department of Corrections, and anyone who wants to visit the grave of a friend or loved one must show identification and register using the same system that applies to prison visits. In 2019, however, it was agreed that New York's Parks and Recreation Department will take over the managing of the cemetery, and work to upgrade the areas and preparing the island for visitors. The takeover is a direct result of the work that the Hart Island Project voluntary organization has been doing since 2011: to uphold the rights of the bereaved and make it easier for people to visit and find information about those buried there.

Meanwhile, in April 2021, the *New York Times* reported from the island, this time about how the number of burials had increased by 300 percent from the previous year. The last time a similar increase had been seen was during the AIDS epidemic, which hit certain parts of New York's population terribly hard. Now there were analyses of the COVID figures which could show that as many as 10 percent of those who had the disease when they died in 2020 were buried in this "potter's field." While the mayor of New York had previously insisted that only deceased persons with no "next of kin" were being sent to Hart Island, stories have surfaced of individuals who searched for their friends and loved ones only to find out to their horror, and all too late, that the person concerned was dead and already buried. Despite what these individual stories suggest, however, the vast majority of those buried on the island (60 percent) do have known surviving family, who for various reasons, primarily a difficult financial situation, choose, or feel compelled, to have the deceased buried at the state's expense, in a mass grave along with 149 others.

Is there another way of looking at these mass graves? Melinda Hunt, who founded the Hart Island Project, believes it is time to break the taboos surrounding the island. Hunt argues that Hart Island is not just an expression of poverty and injustice—"a Dickensian system." On the contrary, she claims, burials here are carried out in an orderly manner. The key to regaining a sense of dignity lies in removing the shame associated with being buried in this way, along with so many other nameless people. To contribute to this process, the Hart Island Project runs a website where those buried on the island can get their names and identities back, thanks to previously unseen burial records that were recently passed on by the Department of Corrections.

Today, anyone who was buried on the island after 1980 can be found by doing a simple search on the website. A person's name, age, and the plot in which they are buried is now freely available information. Relatives, friends, or other interested parties are also invited to contribute to the website with short stories and pictures that can be linked to the buried individuals. An interactive memorial, a platform for collecting stories about the formerly nameless dead.

11

DEATH AS JEWELRY

In Sayaka Murata's short story "A First-Rate Material" (2017), the Japanese author describes a young couple who are about to get married and are planning their life together. They love each other, but they struggle to agree on interiors and furniture—not that hard to recognize for anyone who has tried going from two separate households to a single joint one. But for this couple the problem is more deeply rooted. The groom refuses to have anything made of human material near him. Be it hair, nails, bones, or skin—he will not have it, not as furniture, lamps, kitchen utensils, or clothing. He will not even have his wedding ring made of human teeth. The bride is distraught; her friends have no sympathy for the man's eccentric position, and neither does she. She cannot understand why it is such a big deal for him: "It's sacrilege," he says, "it's crazy", "it's grotesque", "it's cruel!" Would it not be more of a sacrilege to discard such beautiful material when it can be reused, thinks the bride. It is a precious and noble feature of our advanced way of life, she tries to convince her fiancé, that we do not allow the bodies of our dead go to waste, that our own bodies in fact continue to be useful long after we have passed away! "We humans are also materials—and that's wonderful!" To just burn it all would be far more heartbreaking.

The turning point comes when the couple go to visit the groom's family. His father, who he had a difficult relationship with

Death as Jewelry

throughout his childhood, has been dead for several years. However, it turns out that the father's dying wish was for his skin to be made into a beautiful bridal veil—a veil that the groom's mother has looked after, waiting for this happy occasion when their eldest son is to be married. It will of course mean everything to her, and her late husband *in absentia*, that their daughter-in-law wears the veil. The bride is persuaded to try on the veil but is unsure how her fiancé will react. "I felt as though I were standing in the most sacred church in the world," she tells the reader. But instead of ripping the veil from her head, the groom carefully approaches her, and then notices that the veil has the scar he gave his father during a traumatic argument in his teens. He buries his face in the veil and mumbles, "Dad."

If we consider this short story a literary project, it strikes us as borderline science fiction, and what we readers get out of it will probably vary. Are we being invited into a dystopian future where the ideals of innovation and sustainability have gone completely off the rails, and at the expense of all norms and common decency? Or does the story touch upon a basic human desire and need to maintain a connection with our dead; a desire that has always been managed using various forms of physical memorials—objects that help us remember those who left us? Some would say the story has no more relevance than a horror story. But they would be very wrong!

The funeral industry is conservative. You can see it everywhere, in the almost identical black cars, in the black uniforms, all the quiet discretion surrounding the funeral homes. When funeral homes advertise, the language used emphasizes dignity, care, professionalism, and safety. Since no one wants to see photos of coffins, graves, or mournful ceremonies, much less of dead people, the advertising is normally discreet, whether it is a small half-page advert or notice in the parish magazine or local newspaper, or used as the window decoration of the funeral home itself. It could be a lily, a beautiful sculpture, a candle, or perhaps a river representing the flow of life.

It has been like this for as long as we can remember, that is, until a few years ago when we noticed that something was about to happen at the corner of another cemetery slightly further away from our house, just on the other side of the hospital. It may seem strange to have two graveyards so close to each other, but until very recently, Oslo was a city divided by class. And while the graveyard surrounding our house has a working-class profile, the one situated a few hundred yards to the west is more bourgeois.

There were already two funeral homes on this busy and visible corner, which had proven to be entirely unsuitable for any other type of business. In the first window there is a picture of a large, purple flower and the company logo using a classic font. In the second window there is a display of headstones, all gray and somber and roughly the same size, one decorated with a bird, another with a cross. Then, in autumn 2019, a third funeral home called the Final Journey appeared next door.

The only other premises in this row of businesses now belongs to a shop that has held its own against online competitors and still offers the sale and engraving of trophies. Although with it being next to all the funeral homes, you cannot help noticing how the trophies bear a striking resemblance to urns.

While the facades of the two established funeral homes differ only as much as two graphic profiles within the same genre will allow, the Final Journey is immediately different. Its window has a sign saying, in large, white letters: "People are different. We think funerals should be like that too." In the next window there is a picture of a diamond, accompanied by the text "Memorial diamonds from cremation ashes." Cremation ashes, it turns out, are a first-class material, not just for forging into jewelry and swords, as they perhaps were well over 1,000 years ago, but also as the basic ingredient in the most precious of all precious stones—an artificially produced diamond.

The Final Journey is the rebel of the Norwegian funeral industry, and the brainchild of Pia Cyrén. We met Cyrén at the annual convention of the Virke trade organization in 2018. Most colleagues at the convention wear dark suits, although some, in the absence of bereaved relatives, use the opportunity to dress more casually in jeans and a T-shirt. Cyrén, however, is dressed from head to toe in white, a work uniform that makes her immediately stand out from the rest of the attendees. She has manicured nails, carefully styled hair, and glossy lips. She smiles and laughs, occasionally stopping to kiss people on the cheeks before moving quickly on. While the other funeral consultants have perfected the art of anonymous integrity, and the ability to disappear, slip into the background, swallowed by the shadows until needed, Cyrén descends the stairs to the lounge on the ground floor of the conference hotel, and shines like a star.

Her agency is small—it is mostly just her—yet its arrival has caused a huge ripple effect. The Final Journey has a totally new way of approaching funerals. "Serve champagne in the garden," "send a paper lantern up at the end," "give the urn a sea burial," "scatter the ashes on a mountaintop, then ski back down as a group." Cyrén's latest offer lets you send your loved one's ashes into space. For the price of a good headstone—around $2,000—you can have the urn sent up into space attached to a weather balloon. And with the help of a built-in camera, you can follow your loved one's journey into the atmosphere, where the urn will open, spreading the ashes over a vast area before they cascade back to earth, a flake onto the cabin, a flake onto the favorite beach in Greece, one onto the beautiful nearby lake which supplies the water in the tap at home, and billions of other flakes onto billions of other places.

But the most radical offer, in many ways—for which Cyrén and the Final Journey have received the most attention—is the memorial diamond, which is made out of the deceased. "Our memorial diamonds are made from your loved one, and are therefore entirely unique," it says on the website, with a reminder that "diamonds last forever."

Unlike most people in the industry, Pia Cyrén neither was born nor married into the business. She previously worked in sales and product development for the office industry, most recently at the printer company Xerox. There, her main responsibility was for the huge industrial machines used by a handful of professional customers. One of her most important projects at the time was the development of a reusable card for purchasing cigarettes from vending machines.

Cyrén told us how she worked closely with the marketing manager, Johnny, and that after a while this once energetic colleague started becoming increasingly frail. It turned out that he had cancer, and the doctors gave him three months to live. Johnny said that what he wanted most was to keep working for as long as he could. He also wanted to plan his own funeral, or "farewell party," as he called it, which he wanted to be a grand, positive experience for friends and family. His life had been a celebration, and he wanted his funeral to be one too.

Johnny wanted all of the guests to get champagne during the ceremony. He wanted a brass band that would blow the wax out of every ear in the room. And he wanted to deliver his own speech, via a projection on the wall. He also had opinions about what the band should play: "Johnny B. Goode," of course, since his name was Johnny. And "Bad Things," by Jace Everett. That was him, Cyrén told us: everyone should leave the funeral with a smile on their face.

When Johnny explained all this to the various funeral directors, they opposed almost every idea. He was consistently told in a stern, paternalistic voice what was normal, and thus what was acceptable and what could not be done. If he wanted to have champagne at the wake, that could be arranged. But not during the church ceremony or in the chapel. It was quite inappropriate. And the thing with the music, that was something he need not concern himself with. They would consult the bereaved about that when he was dead and choose a hymn.

"I don't think you really understand," he said. "I'm not having a wake, I'm having a farewell party. The last guy to be carried out when everyone is significantly tipsy, will be me. I'm going to be there every step of the way." When Johnny was told that was not possible, he was furious. But he was going to do it anyway. "He was an adult, he'd been an adult for decades and was used to making his own decisions. But when it came to his own death, he was being denied that opportunity," says Cyrén.

What would be the perfect funeral home for someone like Johnny? What people like him needed was flexibility and options. A funeral app maybe? Something totally different from the gray and boring "this is how we usually do it" mentality.

Things went very quickly for Johnny. He did not even get three months, and one Sunday in early spring he died. The following week there was a funeral. As a result of all the problems with the funeral directors, the family chose to do almost everything themselves. The funeral home drove the coffin to the local ceremony room, and that was it. The rest was organized by the family. Johnny's sons, aged nineteen and 21, were the masters of ceremonies.

When the guests arrived, it was almost like arriving at a night-club. The sound of jazz streamed from the open doors. It was a beautiful day with clusters of sprouting daffodils around the trees where the snow had recently melted, and the guests stood outside drinking champagne in the spring sun. And no matter where you turned, Johnny was there. Johnny was full of aphorisms, always with something clever, funny, sharp, or cheeky to say, and quotes were now written on notes attached to sticks poking up from the snow.

Inside, long tables were set for two hundred people, the jazz band played, and there was more champagne. Then came Johnny himself, giving speeches that he had videotaped beforehand. "It was absolutely beautiful. The way it was supposed to be. Just how Johnny wanted it," says Cyrén. "And then I thought there's no point making the damned app that Johnny and I had talked about if you only meet resistance and people who tell you these things can't be done. You can't be dependent on your family having to do it all themselves. So I decided, there and then. I'll do it. I'll start my own funeral home."

Cyrén started interviewing people who knew they were going to die. She found that most people were grief-stricken not just because they were going to pass away, but because they were not going to be around anymore; they would no longer be there for their loved ones. One woman knew that her son was due to celebrate his confirmation the following year, and that she would no longer be around for it. In another instance, a wedding had been planned.

"I was sure that something could be done about these things," says Cyrén. She decided that her funeral home would not just be about the funeral, but also, in a way, about life after death. She named it the Final Journey, instead of choosing the more playful *Trøste og bære* (literally, Comfort and Carry), which she and Johnny had used as a working title while brainstorming. In short, Cyrén's idea was about letting the customer decide. Everything legal should be possible. If you did not want to have the funeral ceremony in a church or chapel, then you could have the commemoration at home, or outside, on the fjord or in the mountains—or at your favorite restaurant. "There's actually no law against bringing a coffin into a restaurant, although it might be more practical to cremate first, and just bring the urn," says Cyrén, laughing.

The diamonds for which Pia Cyrén has become best known are made from cremation ashes. Instead of the urn being buried, or the ashes scattered to the wind (or released into space), the urn and its contents are sent to a company called LifeGem in the Netherlands. There, they separate the pure carbon from the ash. The body of an adult man will produce around 10 pounds (4.5 kg) of ash, which is more than enough to make a diamond. In fact, the largest diamonds LifeGem offers, roughly 1 carat—at a price of €20,000—only use one-fifth of the ash produced. Most people choose far smaller diamonds, however. If you want, you can have several stones made from the same body—perhaps one for each of the deceased's children? The method used to produce the diamonds is a replication of what happens in nature, a technological innovation from the mid-1950s. The carbon is placed in a kind of a pressure chamber where it is subjected to high pressure and temperature. After fourteen months (instead of millions of years), the diamond is ready.

In 2014—after an article in a Christian newspaper mentioned the diamonds that the Final Journey offer—Bishop Halvor Nordhaug strongly criticized what he thought of as an unfortunate development in society. He even said he believed the process to be illegal, a circumvention of both the laws of God and the laws of men.

"What you do is send the ashes to a company abroad, which carries out this diamond process. And you get this gemstone in return. And then grandma has to clear customs on the way back. This is a highly inappropriate process. A withdrawal from the community that is deeply regrettable," Nordhaug thundered. Without intending to, controversies like these attracted even more attention to the Final Journey, and led to a rare, lively discussion in an industry that was otherwise known for cultivating discretion and silence, slowness and conservatism. To date, the Final Journey has sold around three hundred of these ash diamonds, and other, more traditional funeral homes have started offering the same service, although mostly without the same number of sales. When the parameters are conservative, it is hard getting people to choose differently, but for Cyrén, her very trademark is that she offers new things. The Christian sense of community—which is what we have to assume the bishop was referring to—and its ideal of lying safely in the cemetery while awaiting resurrection are no longer dominant.

"I don't think funeral homes should be a kind of extension of the church. That's of course not who we are. We have freedom of religion. People can believe and in general do what they want. But when you die, this freedom is suddenly no longer the same," says Cyrén. "We've been abiding by traditions that people no longer identify with. That everyone has to use the standard white coffin, we recite from a book that means very little to many people, we sing hymns for people who have never sung one themselves in their life when they die. These are traditions that have run their course," she continues. "Customs come and go. I asked one of the old people in the business, the 'dinosaurs' I call them, if he had a Christmas tree at home and he said 'Yes.' Well, 150 years ago, no one but the Germans had Christmas trees. Traditions change all the time."

IF WE TAKE a long-term perspective on human history, we see that traditions come and go, and that what is considered natural and unnatural, "appropriate" and "inappropriate," changes in line with cultural practice and innovation. We have already seen several examples in this book. At the same time, it is interesting to see how some traditions also constantly seem to find ways *back*, managed within new frameworks and other imaginary worlds.

Making industrial diamonds out of deceased loved ones is clearly a new funeral custom. But the fact that the human body is a first-class material for jewelry production and memorabilia is something we have known about, and made use of, for a very long time.

Paul Pettitt, who has worked extensively on the origins of human mortuary practices in archaeological material, writes about two crucial innovations that came at roughly the same time in our prehistory: formalized burial grounds, that is, places where the community can go to bury and commemorate their dead beside other dead; and the circulation of human relics, or remains in the form of jewelry and amulets—something you can carry with you. Among the innumerable human ways of dealing with death, both the bishop's preferred graveyard and Cyrén's diamond solution appear as two equally relevant *and* original possibilities.

Before we learned how to turn ashes into diamonds, however, it was crucial that whatever part of the body one chose to take care of did not rot. Bones, for example—and particularly teeth—last very well and can be relatively easily turned into pendants, beads, and amulets. The jawbone that Malinowski had seen hanging around a widow's neck in the Trobriand Islands in 1918 is still preserved among the objects that the anthropologist took back to London, now in the collection of the British Museum. In the Viking town of Ribe in Denmark, a human skull fragment has been found with a hole drilled from the inside (sometime after the person in question had died, obviously). This pendant does not look like it was ever threaded onto a string—there are no signs of wear in the hole—but the runes carved onto the surface give us some idea about how it was used: they invoke the gods to help against "this pain." Perhaps the person needed relief from a headache, or the pain of longing and grieving for the dead?

Another durable human material is hair. In a purely physical sense, hair is already dead material while attached to the living body, something that makes it less susceptible to decomposition when the body dies. If you remove hair (primarily head hair) from the body, it can last practically forever, under the right circumstances. This was part of the starting point for an extremely widespread jewelry-and-needlework tradition that developed in Europe in the seventeenth century and was at its most popular in the nineteenth century, during the reign of Queen Victoria.

In many cultural-historical museum collections there are examples of so-called hairwork: bracelets, necklaces, brooches, watch straps, rings, and earrings—even flower-like arrangements and framed pictures—all made from knotted human hair. The jewelry and pictures could be made using hair from one or more people. Often, they were made in connection with someone's death. In some cases, they would also consist of hair from different family members, so a person's hair would represent and embody the individual—either singularly or entwined with the hair of others near and dear. Just as Cyrén stresses how cremation diamonds are a unique way to memorialize someone, several authors who look at the tradition of hair jewelry have also highlighted how this form of mourning jewelry literally contains the individual, which makes it a very personal memory of, and about, the person being mourned. To be absolutely sure that the jewelry was made from *your* loved one's hair (and not a random stranger's), women were largely encouraged to learn the art of hairwork themselves. This special form of handicraft became a kind of phenomenon among the upper middle class, and during the nineteenth century several "pattern books" were published containing descriptions of the technique and illustrations of the various patterns you could try.

These books, and the many pieces of hairwork that are preserved from the era, say something about the degree of cultural acceptance there was towards people carrying parts of their friends and loved ones around with them, so close to their own body, as a personal and physical memento. The need to wear or be surrounded by objects that belonged to the deceased says a lot about how people use material culture—things—to remember, not just in an abstract sense but as a way of being able to touch and feel, smell and imagine a small piece of the life we miss. In the article "The Dead Still among Us" (2011), Deborah Lutz describes the tradition of hair jewelry as being part of a tradition of "secular relics," and connects the emergence of this (in historical time) to the dissolution of the Catholic monasteries after the Reformation in 1537. When the monasteries were disbanded, many of the holy relics they had been keeping for the community—such as the body parts, bones, hair, or nails of holy men and women—vanished as well. In a Protestant interpretation of Christianity, and soon a more secularly oriented society, memorial objects and personal "sacred" objects gradually became more important in a private context than in the previously religious community, Lutz argues.

Parts of this mourning fashion have survived. In the Swedish village of Våmhus, all eleven-year-old girls learn to knot hair in school, according to a 2017 TV report. It is important that they learn the skill from an early age, before they start school with children from other parts of the region. This knowledge clearly has to be preserved locally. Våmhus has been known for its hairwork since the 1830s, when the local *hårkullor* (hair maids), women who braided jewelry and ornaments from hair, traveled around Scandinavia and Europe selling their wares. One of the hair maids is said to have been a supplier to the court of Queen Victoria herself. The women of the village apparently specialized in the craft following several years of failed harvests and hunger at the end of the 1700s. By doing so, they helped save the village at a difficult time, and although hunger is no longer knocking on the door in Våmhus, hairwork has become an important, and still practiced, part of its cultural heritage. Most people who want today's *hårkullor* to make bracelets or other jewelry for them send their own hair for production. But one of the hair-workers interviewed for the TV report said she also collected good hair to work with and had two chests full of it—untreated children's hair is the very best, apparently.

In 1945, when Norway's self-proclaimed wartime leader Vidkun Quisling was deposed, imprisoned, and sentenced to death for treason, he wrote a final letter to his wife Maria and attached a lock of his hair. Considering the situation, it was probably the most personal and lasting thing he could leave her in his memory. Perhaps he also knew that a former monarch—Queen Victoria of England— carried a lock of Prince Albert's hair with her for over forty years, from the time of his death in 1861 until she passed away herself in 1901. The gold locket, with the lock of hair behind glass on one side and a photo of Prince Albert on the other, is now part of the Royal Collection of Great Britain. After the queen's death, it was placed in the room in which the prince had died at Windsor Castle. She has been called "the grieving monarch," and some believe that Queen Victoria's insistence on grieving for the rest of her widowed life contributed to the fascination with and sentimentality in the face of death that is often associated with the late Victorians. In a way, the medallion also marks an interesting transition from one form of commemorative material to another, a transition that can be linked partly to the emergence of new knowledge and new ideas around public health, and partly to yet another of the many technological innovations that emerged in this century. Hair ornaments slowly but surely went out of fashion during the latter part of the 1800s, just as photography was becoming an increasingly common way of preserving a final memory of people's loved ones.

The exact visual representation that photography offered was revolutionary and, relatively speaking, far less expensive than the portrait paintings the upper classes would order of themselves. It was also quick to produce. There was no need to sit as a model for hours, preferably over several days, or even weeks. The photograph was a picture taken in the moment—a moment, frozen in time, for eternal memory. If you had never had the opportunity to photograph your loved ones in life, it was therefore not too late to do so in death. On the contrary, it became common to photograph both children and adults in the period between death and the funeral. In many cases, the postmortem photograph (taken after death) was the only existing image of the person concerned, so the opportunity was often taken to also photograph the rest of the family with the recently deceased. The dead person would be made up and dressed,

laid in a coffin, sat in a chair, or propped up next to the relatives—
and would have looked asleep had their eyes not been painted on
after the photograph was developed. In various photo collections
around the world, there are numerous examples of particularly
moving images, of children standing beside their deceased mother,
siblings gathered around the youngest boy, who has died, or the
family portrait of mother and father with the small child between
them—all three of them lying dead in the same coffin.

Death portraits account for the largest group of genre photographs in nineteenth-century America, after the technology was
developed in the 1840s. At a time when photography was still
expensive but equally accessible, postmortem photographs were
one of several services that professional photographers could
offer. This also became a common practice in many other countries, and after a while particularly in rural communities, where the
custom was for the dead to lie on a bed of straw at home before
the funeral. With equipment often being heavy and cumbersome
and the right lighting hard to achieve in private homes, it was also
not unusual to bring the deceased to the photographer's studio.
In 1895 this was prohibited in Austria, which suggests that there
must have been a lot of dead people in photo studios if banning
it was necessary.

The earliest postmortem photographs are often relatively
simple and feature light or dark backgrounds. Later photos often
used more flower arrangements, wreaths, candles, draped fabrics,
and lace. In the USA photographers would advertise their services.
One even wrote an article including "tips and tricks" to remember
before photographing the dead. But as the technology gradually
became more accessible, so the death photograph went out of fashion. By the turn of the new century, it was becoming increasingly

common to have photos taken of yourself and your loved ones while still alive. And if you could have photos of your loved ones smiling and laughing on special and eventually normal occasions, it was no longer as important to frame their death as an eternal memory. Such photos of smiling men and women, girls and boys, can be seen on some of the headstones beyond our fence; immortalized in glass or porcelain beside their names and the words in their memory.

Death portraits gained new relevance when our friend, the painter Lars Elling, lost his father in 2020. As death approached, Elling made sketches of his father which eventually became a portrait. The portrait attracted a lot of attention and set in motion a larger debate about the ethics of publishing a work of art depicting someone who is dead—and who is therefore unable to consent. The father's widow reacted to the death portrait, calling it "offensive, sad and disappointing." It was featured on the evening news and in several newspapers. Experts on ethics and press standards gave their views on the matter. "No one really owns a person's legacy," said law professor Olav Torvund when he was interviewed by Norwegian state TV.

What was most striking for Lars, however, was the reactions from individuals who sent him pictures of their own dead fathers. "They came from Tromsø, from Ljubljana, and what they all had in common was that the sender was a son who thought my father resembled theirs. That his father looked like mine," he later wrote in an essay about the controversy. Which, as Lars explained, is totally natural: when a person dies, the soft tissue relaxes, the cranium rises to the surface—the corpses become similar to each other.

He concludes his essay with a reflection on whether the memory of the person who has died is the same as the person depicted in the image: "My father, whose name was Steinar, no longer has a social security number and permanent residence. He no longer has green eyes and a broken little finger. His face, in all phases of life, is fixed to photographic paper and fleeting pixels in the ether. But he is no more there than [Van Gogh's] haystack or [Magritte's] pipe. My father has become a memory. And a painting."

12

LIVING WITH THE DEAD

When the dense, wet darkness of autumn arrives, the cemetery goes from being an inviting green park to somewhere impenetrable and occasionally hostile. The grounds are brown and soft, covered in dead leaves, a darkness hanging over it. Those who still walk through the cemetery on their way to work do so hurriedly and shivering. The joggers, who during the summer months run laps of the cemetery in an attempt to stave off their own mortality, also gradually disappear. The street that cuts through the cemetery becomes more and more deserted, and those with no choice but to walk here, either to get home or to the hospital, pick up their speed and look back fearfully when they hear someone behind them. When the gardeners are done blowing the leaves into huge piles, and the last trees have been pruned, the burial authority's work ceases too. Except when new graves need digging.

That's how it goes, darker and darker, until the end of October, when night falls before the working day is even over. When we get home, the light from the windows of our house is the only sign of any human presence in the cemetery. What was an attractive green space in the city becomes a dark, spooky place, silent and abandoned.

Then one evening, the light suddenly returns. On the evening before All Saints' Day, the cemetery becomes a sea of candles, hundreds, if not thousands of grave lanterns with their delicate, flickering flames, like phosphorescence on a tropical beach. On the mound behind our house, in the aforementioned memorial garden, the candles are tightly packed like a twinkling crescent of fire. And it stays like that for the following weeks. New lanterns arrive every day, and the candles burn for a long time—some lasting over a week, so they do not need to be replaced very often. We rarely see the people who put them there. It is as if they are lit by invisible beings: elves or ghosts. Towards the end of November there is a little less activity, until Christmas greets us with a veritable ocean of flames, like the days when people held cigarette lighters aloft at rock concerts.

It's pushing it to say that we prefer the bleak, snow-free winter to spring and summer, but one could argue that winter is the time when the cemetery is at its most beautiful. It's also that time of year when people who visit us ask what it's really like to live here. How does it feel to live so close to—yes, in a way, to live *with*—the dead?

The answer is that it feels completely natural. They are there, and we are here, on our respective sides of the fence.

ALL SAINTS' DAY is an ancient holiday with somewhat unclear origins. It may have originated sometime during the Middle Ages, as a way of gathering all the saints who were not important enough to have been given their own commemoration day. There has also been speculation over whether the day originates from Celtic or other pre-Christian mythology.

The holiday has not been officially recognized in Norway since several Catholic holidays were abolished in 1770. Nevertheless, people continued to use the day for visiting graves, dressing up to honor the dead, and to offer the deceased a light in the dark.

In the 2000s, the tradition returned in earnest, this time as an import from America. Halloween, or All Hallow's Eve, is entirely different in both form and content to the pious white light that shines in the autumn darkness. The American version came with a horror-film aesthetic—skulls, fake blood, cobwebs and plastic spiders, and excitable children knocking on doors to offer those inside the choice of "trick or treat." Outside the houses and apartment buildings on all sides of the cemetery you'll see hollowed-out pumpkins with a candle inside—a "jack-o'-lantern," named after the Irish legend of Stingy Jack, who tricked the Devil—and flocks of children, dressed as witches, vampires, and zombies, begging for sweets. (So far, no one has dared venture over to our house for a "trick or treat," and in the evening, the illuminated cemetery is completely deserted.)

In other parts of the world, All Saints' Day is not just for remembering the dead, it is for celebrating them—in a way, as a celebration of death. In Mexico, All Saints' Day is considered one of the highlights of the year. El Día de los Muertos—the Day of the Dead—is a two- or in some cases three-day event, where death comes to town. And in this case no one tries to look away. Far from it.

Shortly after arriving in Tzintzuntzan, a town in the central Mexican state of Michoacán, we hear music from the house next door. It is the day before el Día de los Muertos, which is often called Día de los Inocentes (Day of the Innocents), and the Corral family has gathered relatives from far and wide along with their neighbors and friends. We are also considered part of this group, despite being new arrivals and having no connection to them other than the fact that we've rented a room in the house next door. Their celebration is in memory of sixteen-year-old Aaron, who died of cancer the previous year.

It is hard to imagine anything more tragic than losing a teenager, a boy full of life, who loved basketball and had just started to discover the joys of pretty girls and alcohol. And yet it is hard to imagine a memorial ceremony for a dead child being less mournful and more life-affirming than the one Aaron's family has arranged. Outside the garage, a brass band plays cacophonous, high-tempo music, while songs blast from a nearby stereo system in another corner of the party. It's not clear if the various musicians are actually playing the same melody, or if the drummer really belongs to the band or is just a guest who has had one too many.

On the first floor of the spacious house, an altar has been built. The altarpiece is a wall, several yards wide, consisting of marigolds and a photo of Aaron surrounded by a heart of roses. The rest of the altar is decorated with things he liked when he was alive: biscuits, bananas, wine and tequila, a pizza and a hamburger, pastries, fruit, and corn on the cob, as well as a basketball and several photographs of Aaron with his friends. In the middle of the altar there are several motifs created using salt, corn, and different colored sands. There is Jesus embracing a child, a car, a sandy beach with palm trees, and, last but not least, a picture of a skeleton playing basketball—as Aaron is presumably doing in the world of the dead right now. We are invited to have dinner and a complimentary beer. There is a constant rotation of guests: some get excessively drunk, others sentimental. The only person we meet who doesn't seem cheerful is a cousin of Aaron's who remarks that Aaron is dead, that we will never see him again, and that it is nothing but tragic. At midnight we leave, but we can hear the music playing for several hours afterwards.

Tzintzuntzan has a rich history. On the town's outskirts there are ancient pyramids from the Aztec period, defensive structures, and buildings that probably had important religious significance. The town also has a monastery complex that is dedicated to St. Francis of Assisi and was built to convert the pagan native population. A coffin with a wax figure of Jesus inside is said to have unusual properties, the legs of the figure growing. The coffin has been expanded several times to allow it to accommodate the increasingly long statue.

It is here, and in some of the other central Mexican states, that the tradition of the Day of the Dead has remained strongest. Whether el Día de los Muertos has a Christian origin, or whether it's what remains of an ancient Aztec holiday, is a question Mexicans have been arguing about since the civil war of the 1850s. But there is little doubt that it has become a distinctly Mexican celebration. This very mix of native traditions and Catholic mysticism has resulted in a unique cultural expression which in 2008 was inscribed into UNESCO's List of Intangible Cultural Heritage of Humanity. In recent years the centuries-long tradition has been revived as an increasingly popular attraction for curious tourists, largely thanks to representations in popular culture. When the 2015 James Bond film *Spectre* opened with a huge Day of the Dead parade in Mexico City, there had not been such a parade in the city for as long as anyone could remember—perhaps ever. But the film, and all the attention it brought, breathed life into the celebrations in the capital and throughout the whole country.

The following afternoon, a procession leaves Aaron's family home and goes into town. The altarpiece is carried at the front, and the family and friends walk behind carrying the altar gifts, while the band tries to reproduce the energy it had the night before. The town center is ablaze with life. Thousands of people are out in the streets, some wearing their Sunday best, others wearing skull makeup, many wearing both—and on the ground are scattered millions of flowers.

The road to the town's cemetery looks like it has been set up for a rock festival, and is lined with vendors, barbecues, and improvised makeup stations where for a few pesos you can be transformed into a skull. Occasionally you'll see someone who has chosen their own design—an Alice Cooper face here, a Kiss mask there.

Inside the cemetery, hundreds of thousands of candles cover the graves, nearly all of which are decorated with flower arrangements, pictures, and offerings consisting mostly of food and liquor, but also personal items like razors, embroidery kits, and books. Some of the graves on the poor side of the cemetery are decorated with a simple marigold wreath, a photograph, a bottle of beer, a taco, and a single candle, while on the wealthier side of the cemetery they have entire installations. Some graves have tents erected over them with chairs for the guests. There are dozens of bands playing, often no more than a few yards from each other, much like competing nightclubs at a beach in Florida or Thailand. At one of the graves, we see a family dancing, and in their case, it is clearly the father who has passed away. A large photograph beside the grave, taken many years earlier, shows a handsome but serious middle-aged man. The elderly mother in mourning clothes dances a slow, sad dance with her son to the tunes of frenetic mariachi music. You get the feeling that the son is the embodiment of the father, and when the band finally slows down and plays a slow, quiet song—perhaps *their* song—it becomes too much for the mother. She sits down and weeps a little before continuing the dance. At Aaron's grave, we meet his family again, along with a number of youths, friends of Aaron's drinking beer with their deceased buddy.

The main point with the Day of the Dead is to commemorate. But it is also about something else: that death is not an absolute end to a relationship. The dead are not here, but nor are they *not here*. The Day of the Dead is an opportunity to be temporarily reunited with those who have passed away.

To tempt the soul back to earth, to make the return journey as easy as possible, the family place flowers, candles, and other gifts along the road between the cemetery and their home. This is why they party at the grave, and why the altar in Aaron's parents' living room is decked out with all the things he loved in life, what he liked to eat, and what he liked to do. The party and the effort the family makes represent an opportunity to continue the relationship. The Pixar film *Coco* (2017), which bases much of its plot on the Day of the Dead mythology, depicts this beautifully. It presents the day as an opportunity for the dead, who usually live in another, parallel world, not so different from our own, to cross back over to the world of the living. The requirement for making this crossing is that someone in the world of the living remembers you, that there is an altar somewhere with your picture on it. If there is not, then it means you have been forgotten. You'll then be unable to return, and will vanish into the world of the dead forever. Only when you are forgotten among the living do you die the irrevocable death.

THE IDEA THAT death has several phases, and that it is not complete when the heart stops beating or when the body decomposes, appears in various forms in various cultures.

From prehistory we know many examples of how the dead, and parts of the dead, sometimes seem to have maintained a kind of physical place among the living. In what is considered one of the world's first cities, Çatalhöyük in present-day Turkey, early farmers lived together in their thousands as early as 9,000 years ago. They built their houses from clay, more or less rectangular, and so close together that there were no streets between them. Instead, the inhabitants moved from roof to roof, and each individual house was accessed via a ladder through a hatch in the ceiling. All the everyday chores, such as cooking and craftwork, were carried out downstairs in the largest room, where the furnace was located. On a slightly raised platform, people worked during the day and rested at night. Beneath this platform, they buried their dead.

Archaeological excavations have been going on in Çatalhöyük since the 1960s, and no cemetery has ever been found either around or outside the city. It is clear that burial in the home was the usual practice throughout the city's lifetime. Adults and children, women and men, were all buried like this, and beneath some floors there can be dozens of individuals, or parts of individuals. But this does not mean we are talking about mass graves, or even double or triple graves, for that matter. In Çatalhöyük, most people were buried individually—that is, the floor in each of these houses was dug up at fairly regular intervals so that the recently deceased could be buried with those who had been laid to rest on earlier occasions. Bones from fully or partially skeletonized bodies would be moved when there was a new burial—to make room. Sometimes it appears that in the same course of events, or in other contexts, individual bones and even skulls have been removed from the under-floor graves. Maybe they were moved to other graves, or used in other ritual or social contexts, or laid in the foundations of new buildings (infants in particular seem to have been used like this in the city's renewal). Perhaps they were even used for decoration or display for some reason—just as they are used on the altar during the Day of the Dead? Whatever the case may be, it is clear that everyone who lived in Çatalhöyük also lived with the dead. They must have had a close relationship with death—the dead were there in the house, a part of everyday life.

In the present day, one of the best-known examples of a radically different approach to death, and to when it occurs, can be found among the Torajan people on the Indonesian island of Sulawesi. Dandooro was 86 at the time of his death. Two years later, when the BBC visited his family, instead of Dandooro lying in the ground, they found him lying in a coffin in the middle of the living room.

"How are you today?" asks the son, bringing lunch into the room.

The head of the family is served two meals a day and is offered cigarettes and coffee in between. The grandchildren run about unfazed, playing and fooling around, as if the dead grandfather is actually just taking a nap. Dandooro is consulted about important matters, and visiting family and other guests make a point of greeting him. He is still a full-fledged member of the family.

Although his heart and other organs have not functioned for years, he is not considered dead. It is more like he is sick, a person who needs care and attention. The son has a soft sponge which he uses to wipe the dust off his father's face. There are signs that Dandooro's nose—one of the most delicate parts of the body—has been repaired with what looks like household putty, the same as you might use when fixing a loose kitchen tile. The Toraja have developed their own form of embalming, which at its most basic is a kind of sun drying, but which today can also include the use of modern embalming liquids.

Dandooro is certainly not the only person in the community to remain unburied. Another neighbor has been lying in state in his daughter's house for the last twelve years. We also read about two brothers who shared a bed with their dead grandfather for seven years before eventually burying him. Every morning they would lift him out of bed, put sunglasses on him and prop him up against the wall. The custom does not apply to all Torajans, but to the group who see themselves as "nobles," and is part of what maintains the distinction between them and the ordinary farmers and peasants who descended from slaves.

For those of us used to there being a marked distinction between life and death, this seems alien, and in many ways wholly impractical. And it is hard to accept the Torajans' protracted death rituals without considering the sanitary aspect of having a corpse in the living room. The smell, all of the minor and major considerations you have to take, the inconvenience of no longer being able to use the front room without contemplating what your dead father-in-law thinks about the programming. There is little doubt that the Torajans' mortuary practice is a cultural tradition that has evolved way beyond what can be considered mainstream by the vast majority of people on earth, who—aside from their religious beliefs and traditions, and whether the corpse is buried, burned, or eaten by birds—are all keen on separating the corpse from the living as quickly as possible.

But there is also a practical element to the Torajans' traditions, however impractical they may seem. The funeral itself, when it is finally held, is an elaborate affair by any standard and involves a quite extravagant use of resources. Food is prepared for hundreds of guests; a temporary guest village is built; and pigs and water buffalo are sacrificed to help the dead soul on its way to the underworld. Postponing the final farewell gives a family time to save money until they can afford the festivities. It is also a matter of status. If the deceased was a high-ranking member of the local community, the family will be able to postpone the fall in status, and new generations can add to their own merits while continuing to lean on the prestige of the deceased—who is of course just considered poorly, not dead.

Even after the funeral, it is still not completely over. Deceased relatives are exhumed from their graves, at uneven intervals, for the *Ma'nene* ritual, a cleaning process where the corpse is washed and occasionally has its clothes changed, until the corpse has disintegrated, and the cleaning is no longer possible. A similar ritual is also practiced in Madagascar, in a funerary tradition called *famadihana*, where corpses are dug up and wrapped in silk cloths. Relatives will then dance with the corpse until it is reburied. The custom has been linked to the spread of pneumonic plague, so there have been several attempts to have it banned, without it having ceased completely.

In many cultures, deceased ancestors hold a variety of roles that the living must actively deal with. Even the transition between living and dead has to be managed according to specific rules and norms that apply to both the dead and the living. If the transition is interrupted or disturbed in any way it can lead to hauntings, accidents, an unwanted coalescence of worlds, or simply the lack of a dignified ending or sense of being able to move on. In Norway, we hold memorial services, and funerals where we bury a body or ashes after a specified number of days. In prehistory, and to this day in some parts of the world, the time between the physical death of the body and a person's social death can involve entirely different rituals and activities and sometimes go on for several years or generations. They can be little things, such as what granddad had thought about the changes being made to the family cabin, or part of larger, more formalized decision-making processes. In many African societies, the dead must be consulted during religious rituals or when important decisions are to be made.

In many cases, our proximity to the dead is governed by other considerations that are more about practical issues or necessity than a belief system. A few years ago, we were allowed to enter the catacombs beneath St. Peter's Church, where people have been looking for and, perhaps miraculously, claim to have found the remains of St. Peter. The archaeological excavations have also uncovered a Roman necropolis of mausoleums for wealthy Roman citizens, some of which were as big as houses. When there was a race at the nearby racetrack, the family would sit on the roof eating and drinking while sending food and wine through a pipe down to the dead on the floor below.

The Romans' magnificent tombs cannot, however, compare with the Egyptians' culture of the dead. For thousands of years, since the time of the pharaohs, the Egyptians built extensive necropolises— not just burial grounds, but veritable cities of the dead. While these unique and magnificent structures continue to fascinate and fill us with awe—at both the skill of the construction and the willingness to use resources so recklessly—the pyramids are in reality parts of colossal burial grounds. The pyramids, the royal tombs, are at the center; around them, the mastabas, for the less important royalty and other members of society's upper echelons; and beyond that there were streets and avenues. At Giza, which is located in the desert outside Cairo, as well as the former capital Memphis and in the Luxor Valley, these cities of the dead were covered by sand, preserved, and in more recent times excavated by archaeologists. The tradition of pyramid building came to an end, but not the activity at the heart of the mortuary practice: building for the dead.

When the new city—Cairo—emerged during the first millennium and took over as Egypt's capital under various forms of Islamic government, the tradition of building town-like cemeteries continued, and they eventually became huge. The new religion prescribed simple burials; however, the population retained many of their old burial customs. Beautiful headstones and monuments were not enough for wealthy families, who instead built mausoleums and burial complexes—solid upholders of status, often with several rooms, both tombs for the dead and living spaces that the family could use on days of commemoration. They were originally located away from the city—beyond the floodplains, the thin strip of land along the Nile that was considered habitable. As Cairo grew it started bordering the cemeteries; and as its growth has only continued at an almost explosive rate over the last two centuries, the city has started surrounding them. The cities of the dead now have roads and railway lines built over and through them, and every week, hectic and informal markets are held there after Friday prayers. You will find the same trinket and secondhand stalls as one can elsewhere in the city, along with more specialized vendors selling wild animals like monkeys, falcons, and cobras, and a separate breeder's market for dogs, where—for a small fee, and to amuse the public—owners can bring bitches that are in heat to mate with male dogs that are considered particularly beautiful, large, or aggressive.

People started moving into the necropolises a long time ago, beginning with the caretakers of rich men's tombs, who—with the family's approval—settled in the living areas of the family mausoleums. As payment for tending the grave and moving out when the family came for their ceremonies, they were given a comfortable and safe place to live in a crowded city. Over the years, other groups appeared, living in more informal, slum-like settlements not just between the graves but in the burial chambers themselves. The figures on how many people live within the boundaries of Cairo's necropolis vary enormously, from a few hundred thousand to over 2 million. In his book *Life, Death and Community in Cairo's City of the Dead* (2010), professor and filmmaker Hassan Anash writes about the unique way in which the transformation from grave to residence occurs: headstones and pillars are used as foundations for new houses, and coffins in existing tombs are repurposed as ironing boards, dining tables, and beds.

"A city bursts at the seams," says a poem written by the Egyptian poet Bahaa Jahins. "It spilled over onto its dead,/ How curious you are, O Cairo, With life and death bundled together within you, jumbled up/ Inside you."

There is much deprivation in the necropolis. Living on a burial ground has a stigma attached—much like living in a slum, it is often impractical and dangerous, and large parts of the area lack sanitation, electricity, and clean water. But it is not all deprivation. Over the centuries, the necropolises' surroundings have improved, and the properties have become more sought-after. Those who live in the houses on the hillside, far from the open sewage flowing in the streets, consider themselves privileged, with magnificent views when the smog over the city clears. Attempts to move residents from the necropolis have been met with resistance. Although the goal is to improve the population's living standards by moving people from informal settlements to newly created residential areas with better public services, health care, and education, the move also means the severing of social ties, and the residents having to swap something familiar for something unknown. "We live better than many people," says a woman interviewed by the Egyptian newspaper *Al-Ahram*. "We live in a small villa with walls, a roof and a beautiful garden. Many people in the nicer areas don't even have that."

THE DAILY REMINDER of death's existence, which we get from seeing the headstones and the funerals taking place beyond our fence, has become a part of our lives. We see death coming, new graves being dug and filled. We can be fascinated and amazed by funeral customs, whether they are those we see around us, those practiced elsewhere, or the many different practices we know from the past. But these things cannot fully prepare us for death itself when it approaches.

The summer before we finished writing this book, a friend, the wife of a colleague at Geitmyra, died of cancer. Marte never reached forty years old. As well as her husband and many friends she also left behind her seven-year-old son, Simon.

She was cremated at the city crematorium at Alfaset, and as with the other parts of the process, Simon was present. He had been with her in hospital, he had felt her skin when it had gone cold, and he had watched the coffin enter the cremation furnace and catch fire before the doors closed. In her hand Marte held a stone that Simon had once given her. It was glossy and dark and shaped like a heart. When Simon got the stone back a few days later, it had turned light gray.

Marte was given her own grave at Oslo North Cemetery. The urn interment took place on what would have been her fortieth birthday, under a gravestone that has been sandblasted and reused from an old grave in Oslo West Cemetery, and with a willow tree planted in her ashes. When the family held a memorial service at Geitmyra, it was raining. Pia Cyrén arrived early, as always dressed in white. She had created an online memorial which has since been filled with hundreds of tributes—some from close family and friends who had followed Marte her entire life, some from classmates and acquaintances who had lost contact but remembered good times, and others from former colleagues and employers. One of the writers had only met Marte once, at a wedding; another had spent a week with her on a yoga retreat.

In the same place her wedding dinner had been held a few years earlier—also in the pouring rain—her newly widowed husband welcomed friends and acquaintances. There was good food and drink, just as Marte had wanted, along with moving speeches and beautiful music. The guests tried their best to avoid getting drenched by the rain when crossing the square.

Before the guests went home, they received a small gift from Marte, something to remember her by: a cutting from a beautiful potted plant that had been growing at home in her living room, a painted nettle—*Solenostemon scutellarioides*—with purple and green leaves which had been divided into many small cuttings that would now grow on the windowsills of those who had been close to her. It was indisputable and painful, incomprehensible and relentless, shocking—and at the same time the most natural thing in the world.

It therefore ended as it had to end: death came over to our side of the fence. We cried and mourned. We wished more than anything that it hadn't struck her the way it had, not her, not then. But we were happy to have taken part in the farewell, that it had taken place right here, that everything was so close to us. Because no matter how else we might think about it, death is a part of life.

Sources

Since this is not an academic book, we decided against including footnotes. However, for those who want to use this book as a starting point for further reading, we have compiled a list of some of the literature that informed our own writing.

General Sources

Paul Pettitt has worked with early human mortuary practices for many years, and *The Palaeolithic Origins of Human Burial* (London and New York, 2011) is a very good and comprehensive academic review of the subject.

One of the most up-to-date summaries in recent years concerning the periods just before and during the Viking Age in Scandinavia is Neil Price's fabulous book *The Children of Ash and Elm: A History of the Vikings* (London, 2020). Here Price also writes a lot about the world of the dead, which is something we have greatly benefited from in the parts of this book where we describe finds and practices from the Late Iron Age.

Sue Black is a professor of anatomy and forensic medicine and writes engagingly about this field for a general audience in *All That Remains: A Life in Death* (New York, 2018).

English author Jessica Mitford's *The American Way of Death* [1963] (New York, 1998), a book about the American funeral industry, lifted the veil of an industry that had until then operated using secret codes and hidden sales practices. It is a classic.

British anthropologist Nigel Barley's book *Grave Matters* (New York, 1995) is an essayistic review of the diversity of burials that is sometimes thought-provoking, sometimes hysterically funny, and richly peppered with anecdotes about different burial customs.

Countless books and articles have been written about the grave robbers that plagued Great Britain and the United States in the 1800s. One such account, which is based on the most extensive documentation and also depicts the society around these personalities, is Sara Wise's *The Italian Boy: Murder and Grave-Robbery in 1830s London* (London, 2004).

One of the main contributors to the growing interest in mortuary practices in recent years is funeral director, blogger, YouTuber, and author Caitlin Doughty. Her project is partly about demystifying death, and partly about fighting to establish new mortuary practices. See her books *Smoke Gets in Your Eyes and Other Lessons from the Crematory* (New York and London, 2015), and *From Here to Eternity: Traveling the World to Find the Good Death* (New York and London, 2017).

Thomas Laqueur has written a very comprehensive book about human remains from a cultural-historical perspective, from antiquity to the present day: *The Work of the Dead: A Cultural History of Mortal Remains* (Princeton, NJ, and London, 2015). It has been especially useful for our understanding of the historical development of modern cremation.

Norwegian archaeologist Terje Østigård has written extensively about cremation practices in both archaeological and contemporary contexts. His contribution to the authoritative *Oxford Handbook of the Archaeology of Death and Burial*, ed. Liv Nilsson Stutz and Sarah Tarlow (Oxford, 2013), "Cremations in Culture and Cosmology," was an especially useful starting point for us. The book also contains a number of other interesting scientific articles on death and burial, from an archaeological perspective.

Finally, the industry magazine *Gravplassen* (The Cemetery) is a rich source of news about everything happening within the Norwegian funeral industry: https://gravplassen.no.

SOURCES BY CHAPTER

1 IN THE BEGINNING THERE WAS THE FUNERAL

Carbonell, Eudald, and Marina Mosquera, "The Emergence of a Symbolic Behaviour: The Sepulchral Pit of Sima de los Huesos, Sierra de Atapuerca, Burgos, Spain," *Human Palaeontology and Prehistory*, C. R. Palevol, v/12 (2006), pp. 155–60

The First Europeans: Treasures from the Hills of Atapuerca, exh. cat., Junta Castilla y León and the American Museum of Natural History (2003)

Surugue, Lea, "Why This Paleolithic Burial Site Is So Strange (and So Important)," *Sapiens*, February 22, 2018, www.sapiens.org

Trinkaus, Erik, and Alexandra P. Buzhilova, "Diversity and Differential Disposal of the Dead at Sunghir," *Antiquity*, xcii/361 (2018), pp. 7–21, https://doi.org/10.15184/aqy.2017.223

2 DEATH AS A PRACTICAL PROBLEM

Doughty, Caitlin, *Will My Cat Eat My Eyeballs? And Other Questions about Dead Bodies* (New York, 2019)

Håvardsen, Tor-Håkon Gabriel, *En seksti under. Alt om dødsfall, likhenting, forråtnelse og en begravelsesagents liv* [Six Feet Under: All about Death, Corpse Retrieval, Decomposition and Life as an Undertaker] (Oslo, 2019)

Roach, Mary, *Stiff: The Curious Lives of Human Cadavers* (New York, 2003)

3 PACKED IN PLASTIC

Aldhouse-Green, Miranda, *Bog Bodies Uncovered: Solving Europe's Ancient Mystery* (London, 2015)

Alsvik, Bård, "Døden i Christiania. Begravelsesvesenet i forrige århundre [Death in Christiania: The Funeral Service in the Last Century]," TOBIAS, iv/98 (1998), www.oslo.kommune.no, accessed July 21, 2021

Bukkemoen, Grethe Bjørkan, and Kjetil Skare, "Humans, Animals and Water: The Deposition of Human and Animal Remains in Norwegian Wetlands," *Journal of Wetland Archaeology*, xviii/1 (2018), pp. 35–55, https://doi.org/10.1080/14732971.2018.1459264

Enerstvedt, Vidar, and Javad Moghimi-Parsa (photographer), "Slik bryter de ned gamle plastsvøpte lik [How Old Plastic-Wrapped Corpses are Broken Down]," VG, June 17, 2013, www.vg.no

Holst, Mads Kähler, Jan Heinemeier, Ejvind Hertz, et al., "Direct Evidence of a Large Northern European Roman Period Martial Event and Post-Battle Corpse Manipulation," PNAS, cxv/23 (June 2018), pp. 5920–25, https://doi.org/10.1073/pnas.1721372115

"Human Fat Candles and Soap," *Scientific American*, October 30, 1852, www.scientificamerican.com, accessed August 12, 2021

Jervell, Ellen Emmerentze, "Grave Problem: Nothing Is Rotting in the State of Norway," *Wall Street Journal*, October 10, 2013, www.wsj.com

Krüger, Frida J., and Erlend Lånke Solbu, "Av jord er du kommet [Ashes to Ashes]," NRK, July 16, 2019, www.nrk.no

O'Sullivan, Muiris, and Liam Downey, "Bog Butter: Why Was It Buried?," *Archaeology Ireland*, xxxiii/2 (Summer 2019), pp. 27–9

Paris Catacombs, www.catacombes.paris.fr/en, accessed August 12, 2021

Reade, Benedicte, "Bog Butter: A Gastronomic Perspective," in *Wrapped and Stuffed Foods: Proceedings of the Oxford Symposium on Food and Cookery 2012*, ed. Mark McWilliams (Oxford, 2013)

Riseng, Per Magnus, "Maren, hvem var du? [Maren, who were you?]," *A-magasine*, October 18, 2019, www.aftenposten.no

Stolze, Dolly, "Soap on a Bone: How Corpse Wax Forms," *Atlas Obscura*, February 17, 2014, www.atlasobscura.com

Tacitus, *Agricola and Germania*, trans. Harold Mattingly (London, 2010)

4 THE BUSINESS OF DEATH

Black, Anetta, "Objects of Intrigue: Diary of a Body Snatcher," *Atlas Obscura*, January 13, 2013, www.atlasobscura.com

Chamberlain, Andrew, and Michael Parker Pearson, *Earthly Remains: The History and Science of Preserved Human Bodies* (New York, 2001)

Hopstock, H., *Det anatomiske institut: 23. januar 1815–23. januar 1913* [The Anatomical Institute: 23 January 1815–23 January 1913], memorandum from the anatomical institute, commissioned by Aschehoug's bookstore in Christiania, 1914

Jacobson, Molly McBride, "A Beginner's Guide to Body Snatching," *Atlas Obscura*, January 26, 2017, www.atlasobscura.com

Laderman, Gary, *Rest in Peace: A Cultural History of Death and the Funeral Home in Twentieth-Century America* (New York, 2003)

Lindhagen, Marina Prusac, ed., *Emotions in Antiquity and Ancient Egypt*, exh. cat., Museum of Cultural History, University of Oslo (2020)

Lovejoy, Bess, "The Gory New York City Riot that Shaped American Medicine," *Smithsonian Magazine*, June 17, 2014, www.smithsonianmag.com

Museum of Cultural History, University of Oslo, "Mumien lever—evig liv i det gamle Egypt [The Mummy Lives—Eternal Life in Ancient Egypt]," www.khm.uio.no, accessed August 10, 2021

Pietila, Antero, "In Need of Cadavers, 19th-Century Medical Students Raid Baltimore's Graves," *Smithsonian Magazine*, October 25, 2018, www.smithsonianmag.com

Smithsonian Institution, Anthropology Outreach Office, "Egyptian Mummies," Smithsonian National Museum of Natural History, www.si.edu, accessed August 10, 2021

Walsh, Brian, "When You Die, You'll Probably Be Embalmed. Thank Abraham Lincoln for That," *Smithsonian Magazine*, November 1, 2017, www.smithsonianmag.com

Webster, Robert D., *Does This Mean You'll See Me Naked? Field Notes from a Funeral Director* (Naperville, IL, 2011).

5 CHOOSING A COFFIN

Breuning-Madsen, Henrik, and Mads K. Holst, "Recent Studies on the Formation of Iron Pans around the Oaken Log Coffins of the Bronze Age Burial Mounds of Denmark," *Journal of Archaeological Science*, 25 (1998), pp. 1103–10

Frei, Karin Margarita, Ulla Mannering, Kristian Kristiansen, et al., "Tracing the Dynamic Life Story of a Bronze Age Female," *Scientific Reports*, v/1 (2015), https://doi.org/10.1038/srep10431

Jensen, Jørgen, "De forunderlige egekister [The Amazing Oak Coffins]," *Danmarks Oldtid* (2004), https://danmarksoldtid.lex.dk

"Regulations for the Graveyards, Cremation and Burials Act," https://lovdata.no, accessed August 18, 2021

Secretan, Thierry, *Going into Darkness: Fantastic Coffins from Africa* (London, 1995)

Stople, Eirik, "Gravlegging etter muslimsk skikk [Burial According to Muslim tradition]," *Gravplassen*, 4 (2018), https://gravplassen.no

Tschumi, Regula, *The Buried Treasures of the Ga: Coffin Art in Ghana* (Berne, 2014)

6 DUST TO DUST

Bang-Andersen, Sveinung, "Svarthålå på Viste—boplass i 6000 år [Vistehola—a Settlement for 6,000 Years]," *AmS-småtrykk*, 13 (1983)

Bergsvik, Knut Andreas, and Ingebjørg Storvik, "Mesolithic Caves and Rockshelters in Western Norway," in *Caves in Context: The Cultural Significance of Caves and Rockshelters in Europe*, ed. Knut Andreas Bergsvik and Robin Skeates (Oxford, 2012), pp. 22–38

Boethius, Adam, Knut Andreas Bergsvik, and Björn Nilsson, "Knowledge from the Ancient Sea—a Long-Term Perspective of Human Impact on Aquatic Life in Mesolithic Scandinavia," *The Holocene*, xxx/5 (2020), pp. 632–45

Brøgger, Anton Wilhelm, *Vistefundet. En ældre stenalders kjøk- kenmødding fra Jæderen* [The Viste Discovery: An Ancient Stone Age Kitchen Midden from Jæderen] (Stavanger, Norway, 1908)

Buggeland, Sven A., and Gøran Bohlin (photographer), "Mykere Milano. De siste trendene innen møbeldesign [Soft Milan: The Latest Trends in Furniture Design]," *vg*, April 12, 2003

Capsula Mundi, www.capsulamundi.it/en, accessed August 12, 2021

Lee, Jae Rhim, "My Mushroom Burial Suit," *TED-Global* (July 2011), www.ted.com

Løvik, Hanne, "Billa var utdødd fra Norge i over 100 år, men så besøkte Magne den gamle kirkegården i Tønsberg [Beetle Was Extinct in Norway for Over 100 Years, but then Magne Visited the Old Cemetery in Tønsberg]," *ABC Nyheter*, April 8, 2017, www.abcnyheter.no

Recompose, https://recompose.life/who-we-are, accessed August 12, 2021

7 UP IN SMOKE

Messel, Nils, ed., *Emanuel Vigeland*, exh. cat., Vigeland Museum, Oslo (1999)

Dittrick, Howard, "Notes and Queries," *Journal of the History of Medicine and Allied Sciences*, III/1 (Winter 1948), pp. 161–71, available online at www.jstor.org

Gansum, Terje, "Role the Bones—from Iron to Steel," *Norwegian Archaeological Review*, XXXVII/1 (2004), pp. 41–57

Grønnestad, Kjetil, "Stadig flere velger kremasjon [More and More People Are Choosing Cremation]," *Gravplassen*, March 15, 2021, https://gravplassen.no

—, "Rekordstor økning av antallet kremasjoner i Norge [Record Numbers of Cremations in Norway]," *Gravplassen*, March 18, 2021, https://gravplassen.no

Hartzman, Marc, "Proper Care for the Not-Quite-Dead-Yet: The London Association for the Prevention of Premature Burial," September 25, 2017, www.weirdhistorian.com

Kirby, Alex, "Animal Disposal Row Intensifies," BBC *News*, April 4, 2001, http://news.bbc.co.uk

Kremer, William, "Dissolving the Dead," BBC, May 22, 2017, WWW.BBC.CO.UK

Meier, Allison C., "The Fear of Being Buried Alive (and How to Prevent It)," JSTOR *Daily*, October 31, 2019, https://daily.jstor.org

Norwegian Cremation Association/Norwegian Association for Cemetery Culture, "Kremasjonsstiftelse. Litt av forhistorien [The Norwegian Cremation Foundation: A Bit of History]," https://gravplasskultur.no, accessed July 27, 2021

Pallis, C. A., "Death," in *Encyclopedia Britannica*, www.britannica.com, accessed August 12, 2021

Pearson, Mike Parker, *The Archaeology of Death and Burial* (College Station, TX, 2000)

Powys, Llewelyn, "Body Snatchers," *Powys Journal*, 6 (1996), pp. 207–13, available online at www.jstor.org

"Resomation: Natural Water Cremation," https://resomation.com/about, accessed August 11, 2021

Snorri Sturluson, *Heimskringla: The Chronicle of the Kings of Norway*, trans. Samuel Laing (Prague, 2018)

Tarazano, D. Lawrence, "People Feared Being Buried Alive So Much They Invented These Special Safety Coffins," *Smithsonian Magazine*, October 26, 2018, www.smithsonianmag.com

The Vatican, "Instruction *Ad resurgentum cum Christo* Regarding the Burial of the Deceased and the Conservation of the Ashes in the Case of Cremation" (2016), www.vatican.va

8 PIECEMEAL AND DIVIDED

Aldred, Jessica, "Banned Livestock Drug Continues to Threaten India's Vultures, Conservationists Warn," *The Guardian*, September 6, 2011, www.theguardian.com

Associated Press, "Zoroastrian Funeral Rites Arouse Anger in India," NBC *News*, September 8, 2006, www.nbcnews.com

Bratberg, Terje, "Stein—gård i Hole [Stein—Farm in Hole]," *Store norske lexicon*, https://snl.no, accessed August 2, 2021

Duin, Johannes J., "Olavsrelikvien i St. Olav domkirke: Helligdomsarmen [Olav's Relic in St. Olav's Cathedral: The Sacred Arm]," in *Streiftog i norsk kirkehistorie 1450–1880. En samling artikler* [Moments in Norwegian Church History 1450–1880: A Collection of Articles] (Oslo, 1984), available online at www.katolsk.no, accessed August 11, 2021. Originally printed in *St. Olav katolsk tidsskrift*, 67 (1955), pp. 350–53.

—, "Hellig Olavs legeme i Trondheim [The Body of Saint Olav in Trondheim]," in *Streiftog i norsk kirkehistorie 1450–1880. En samling artikler* [Moments in Norwegian Church History 1450–1880: A Collection of Articles] (Oslo, 1984), available online at www.katolsk.no, accessed August 11, 2021. Originally printed in *St. Olav katolsk tidsskrift*, 67 (1955), pp. 316–17.

Ebenstein, Joanna, ed., *Morbid Anatomy Anthology* (New York, 2015)

—, ed., *Death: A Graveside Companion* (London, 2017)

Johari, Aarefa, "How a New Prayer Hall Is Changing Funeral Patterns in Mumbai's Parsi Community," April 27, 2016, https://scroll.in

Koudounaris, Paul, *Heavenly Bodies: Cult Treasures and Spectacular Saints from the Catacombs* (London, 2013)

—, *Memento Mori: The Dead among Us* (London, 2015)

Lovejoy, Bess, *Rest in Pieces: The Curious Fates of Famous Corpses* (New York and London, 2016)

Malinowski, Bronisław, and Havelock Ellis, *The Sexual Life of Savages in North-Western Melanesia: An Ethnographic Account of Courtship, Marriage, and Family Life among the Natives of the Trobriand Islands, British New Guinea* (New York and London, 1929)

"Mimizuka, Kyoto, Japan," *Atlas Obscura*, November 7, 2010, www.atlasobscura.com

Nair, Manoj R., "Parsi Prayer Hall at Mumbai Crematorium: Success or Failure?," *Hindustan Times*, February 24, 2019, www.hindustantimes.com

Oleksiak, Wojciech, "Chopin's Gravest Fear," July 14, 2014, https://culture.pl

"Paidusts in the Pandemic," *Parsiana*, July 7, 2020, www.parsiana.com

"Parsiana: The Global Zoroastrian Link Medium," www.parsiana.com, accessed August 12, 2021

Ringvej, Mona, *Landet mot nord* [The Land to the North] (Oslo, 2020)

Russell, James R., "Burial III: In Zoroastrianism," *Encyclopaedia Iranica*, https://iranicaonline.org, accessed August 12, 2021

Snorri Sturluson, *Heimskringla: The Chronicle of the Kings of Norway*, trans. Samuel Laing (Prague, 2018)

Steenhoff, Eirik, "Jakten på Olavsrelikvien [The Hunt for Olav's Relic]," *Catholic Church*, November 10, 2017, www.katolsk.no

Woodyard, Chris, *The Victorian Book of the Dead* (Dayton, OH, 2014)

9 A MONUMENT TO THE DEAD

Bill, Jan, "The Ship Graves on Kormt — and Beyond," in *Royal Graves and Sites at Avaldsnes and Beyond*, ed. Dagfinn Skre (Berlin, 2019), pp. 305–92

—, and Aoife Daly, "The Plundering of the Ship Graves from Oseberg and Gokstad: An Example of Power Politics?," *Antiquity*, LXXXVI/333 (2012), pp. 808–24, http://antiquity.ac.uk

Cockroft, Steph, "Millionaire Property Developer who used Children's Gravestones," *Daily Mail*, August 18, 2015, www.dailymail.co.uk

Ertesvåg, Oda Ruggesæter, "Dronning Margrethes gravmonument ferdig etter 15 års arbeid [Queen Margrethe's Grave Monument Finished after 15 Years of Work]," NRK, April 24, 2018, www.nrk.no

Gansum, Terje, "The Riddle of Oseberg," *Living History*, 6 (2004), pp. 33–7

—, and Thomas Risan, "Oseberghaugen— en stratigrafisk historie [Oseberg-haugen—a Stratigraphic History]," *Vestfoldminne* (Vestfold, 1998/9), pp. 60–72

Gjerpe, Lars Erik, "Hvem er begravd på Gulli? [Who Is Buried at Gulli?]," in *Hauglagt—vikingenes gravskikk på Gulli* [Hauglagt—the Viking Burial Customs at Gulli], exh. cat., Museum of Cultural History, University of Oslo (2011), pp. 10–14

Grund, Jens, "Utilfreds Prins Henrik vil ikke begraves sammen med dronning Margrethe [Unhappy Prince Henrik Will Not Be Buried with Queen Margrethe]," BT, August 3, 2017, www.bt.dk

Holck, Per, "The Oseberg Ship Burial, Norway: New Thoughts on the Skeletons from the Grave Mound," *European Journal of Archaeology*, IX/2–3 (2006), pp. 185–210, https://doi.org/10.1177/1461957107086123

"Ibn Fadlans reisebeskrivelse [Ibn Fadlan's Travelogue]," www.norgeshistorie.no, accessed August 3, 2021

Museum of Cultural History, University of Oslo, "Oseberg," www.khm.uio.no, accessed August 11, 2021

Spence, Kate, "Ancient Egyptian Chronology and the Astronomical Orientation of Pyramids," *Nature*, CDVIII (2000), pp. 320–24, https://doi.org/10.1038/35042510

Smithsonian Institution, Anthropology Outreach Office, "The Egyptian Pyramid," Smithsonian National Museum of Natural History, www.si.edu, accessed August 3, 2021

Winkler, Andreas, "How the Ancient Egyptian Economy Laid the Groundwork for Building the Pyramids," *The Conversation*, November 27, 2018, https://theconversation.com

10 THE EMPTY AND NAMELESS GRAVE

Department of Corrections, City of New York, "Hart Island," www1.nyc.gov, accessed August 11, 2021

Hagesæther, Pål Vegard, and Tor Stenersen (photographer), "Jakten på Jeanette er over [The Hunt for Jeanette Is Over]," *A-magasinet*, November 30, 2020, www.aftenposten.no

"The Hart Island Project," www.hartisland.net, accessed August 11, 2021

Kiernan, Ben, *Blood and Soil: A World History of Genocide and Extermination from Sparta to Darfur* (New Haven, CT, 2009)

Kilgannon, Corey, "As Morgues Fill, NYC to Bury Some Virus Victims in Potter's Field," *New York Times*, April 10, 2020, www.nytimes.com

Loe, Louise, Angela Boyle, Helen Webb, and David Score, *"Given to the ground": A Viking Age Mass Grave on Ridgeway Hill, Weymouth* (Oxford, 2014)

New York City Council, "Hart Island," https://council.nyc.gov, accessed August 11, 2021

Slotnik, Daniel E., "Up to a Tenth of New York City's Corona Virus Dead May Be Buried in a Potter's Field," *New York Times*, March 25, 2021, www.nytimes.com

Wangen, Vivian, *Gravfeltet på Gunnarstorp i Sarpsborg, Østfold. Et monument over dødsriter og kultutøvelse i yngre bronsealder og eldste jernalder* [The Burial Site at Gunnarstorp in Sarpsborg, Østfold: A Monument of Death Rites and Cult Practices in the Late Bronze Age and Early Iron Age], Norske Oldfunn XXVII (Oslo, 2009)

11 DEATH AS JEWELRY

Bjørdal, Sondre, "Vil sende legemet til himmels [Will Send the Body to Heaven]," *Vårt Land*, November 19, 2019, www.vl.no

Carlsen, Marianne Rustad, and Ida Yasin Andersen, "Teikna faren på dødsleiet—enke meiner det er uetisk [Drew Father on His Deathbed—Widow Thinks It's Unethical]," NRK, September 17, 2020, www.nrk.no

Elling Lars, "Dette er ikke en pipe [This Is Not a Pipe]," *Aftenposten*, October 6, 2020, www.aftenposten.no

Eriksen, Marianne Hem, "'Body-Objects' and Personhood in the Iron and Viking Ages: Processing, Curating, and Depositing Skulls in Domestic Space," *World Archaeology*, LII/1 (2020), pp. 103–19, https://doi.org/10.1080/00438243.2019.1741439

Gilje, Caroline Teinum, and Jan Arild Holbek, "Gjør de døde om til diamanter [Turning the Dead into Diamonds]," *Vårt Land*, December 11, 2014, www.vl.no

Glanville, Marte, "Døden i bilder [Death in Pictures]," *Kvinneguiden*, November 23, 2014, www.klikk.no

Grindland, Kari, "*Post mortem-fotografier. Noen skjebner fra Smaalenenes amt* [Post-Mortem Photographs]," in *Bildet lever! Bidrag til norsk fotohistorie 6*, ed. Roger Erlandsen, Vegard Skuseth Halvorsen, and Kåre Olsen (Oslo, 1992), pp. 65–80

Hallam, Elizabeth, and Jenny Hockey, "Visualizing Death: Making Memories from Body to Image," in *Death, Memory and Material Culture* (Oxford and New York, 2001), pp. 129–54

"Hårarbeid [Hair Work]," https://digitaltmuseum.no, accessed August 7, 2021

"Human Remains: Ornament," place of origin: Trobriand Islands; acquisition date: 1922, British Museum, www.britishmuseum.org, accessed August 7, 2021

Little, Becky, "Trendy Victorian-Era Jewelry Was Made from Hair," *National Geographic*, February 11, 2016, www.nationalgeographic.com

Lutz, Deborah, "The Dead Still among Us: Victorian Relics, Hair Jewelry, and Death Culture," *Victorian Literature and Culture*, XXXIX/1 (2011), pp. 127–42, available online at www.jstor.org

Murata, Sayaka, "A First-Rate Material," trans. Ginny Tapley Takemori, in *Freeman's: The Future of New Writing*, ed. John Freeman (New York, 2017), pp. 91–105

"Queen Victoria's Locket, *c.* 1861," Royal Collection Trust: RCIN 65301, www.rct.uk, accessed August 8, 2021

Seim, Marie Fongaard, "Døden på museum [Death at the Museum]," June 14, 2012, https:/norskfolkemuseum.no

Wisløff, Lisa Malvina, and Vera Kvaal, "Lager smykker av menneskehår [Making Jewelry from Human Hair]," NRK, February 20, 2017, www.nrk.no

12 LIVING WITH THE DEAD

Andah, Hassan, *Life, Death and Community in Cairo's City of the Dead* (Bloomington, IN, 2010)

Bennett, Amanda, "When Death Doesn't Mean Goodbye," *National Geographic*, March 11, 2016, www.nationalgeographic.com

Boz, Başak, and Lori D. Hager, "Living above the Dead: Intramural Burial Practices at Çatalhöyük," in *Humans and Landscapes of Çatalhöyük: Reports from the 2000–2008 Seasons*, ed. Ian Hodder, vol. XLVII (London, 2013), pp. 413–40, available online at www.jstor.org

El-Rashdi, Sarah, "Tales from Cairo's Living City of the Dead," https://english.ahram.org.eg, March 21, 2013

"My Father Died Two Years Ago but Still Lives with Us," from the radio documentary "Living with the Dead," BBC, April 18, 2017, www.bbc.co.uk

Sayoga, Putu, "In Indonesia, a Blurred Boundary between the Living and the Dead," *New York Times*, December 14, 2020, www.nytimes.com

Sieber, Claudio, "Cleaning the Dead: The Afterlife Rituals of the Torajan People," *The Guardian*, October 13, 2017, www.theguardian.com

Sims, David, *Understanding Cairo: The Logic of a City Out of Control* (Cairo and New York, 2010)

UNESCO Intangible Cultural Heritage, "Indigenous Festivity Dedicated to the Dead," https://ich.unesco.org, accessed August 12, 2021

Acknowledgments

While working on the *Living with the Dead*, we have spoken to many people who have helped us greatly by sharing their experiences and answering all our questions. Every part of this book has benefited from the knowledge and insight gained during these interviews and conversations. We would like to especially thank Stein Olav Hohle, former director of Oslo Cemeteries Office, who has taken us on several tours not just around our "own" cemetery but around many of the city's other cemeteries. Having been employed by the Oslo Cemeteries Office throughout his entire working life, Stein Olav has an overview, an "institutional memory," and not least a personal interest in the field which we are very happy to have been able to share with him.

We have also been helped enormously by the interviews and conversations with the professionals and individuals who will now be mentioned in the order in which they are presented in the book:

José Miguel Carretero Díaz—head of the Laboratory of Human Evolution at Universidad de Burgos, who spent half of his birthday showing us around the excavation sites of Atapuerca

Freddy Hultgren—owner and general manager of Aker Funeral Directors since 1993

Gunnar Hammersmark—director of the trade organization Virke, and a veteran in the industry. Gunnar likes to entertain at professional social functions where he has earned the nickname "The Sinatra of Death"

Emerson Skeens (Babu)—a good friend who welcomed us on countless visits to Zanzibar. He was organizing his own funeral when Andreas flew down there to say a final goodbye. Babu died a few months later

Kudjoe Affutu—one of Ghana's, and therefore the world's, most renowned fantasy coffin makers, who welcomed us and showed us around when we visited the country

Teshie Nungua—fantasy coffin maker in Ghana. Son of Kane Kwei, Ghana's other most famous fantasy coffin maker

Paa Joe—fantasy coffin maker

Raoul Bretzel—founder and designer at Capsula Mundi

Katrina Spade—one of the pioneers of America's so-called "alternative death movement" and founder of Recompose

Pia Cyrén—founder and owner of the Final Journey

In addition to many other employees at Oslo Cemeteries Office, along with employees at the Oslo North Cemetery, Oslo East Cemetery, and the crematorium at Alfaset.

We also greatly appreciate the trust and acceptance shown to us by the bereaved who invited us to funerals and commemorations related to their deceased loved ones:

Jobi Jaboa and family in Ghana

The Corral family in Mexico

Eivind Løvdal and Simon in Oslo